THE
KINGS & QUEENS
OF
ENGLAND

THE NATIONAL PORTRAIT GALLERY HISTORY OF

THE
KINGS & QUEENS
OF
ENGLAND

DAVID WILLIAMSON

BARNES
&NOBLE
BOOKS
NEW YORK

To the memory of Johan Danielsson
1952-97

This edition published by Barnes & Noble Books in 2003
by special arrangement with Konecky & Konecky

ISBN: 0-7607-4678-8

Printed and bound in Korea

Frontispiece:
Queen Elizabeth, the Duke of Edinburgh and their grandchildren,
Prince William, Prince Harry and Peter and Zara Phillips
photographed by Yousuf Karsh, 1987

The dates given in family trees and section headings refer to reign, not birth and death.

CONTENTS

*1. The 10th-century King Edgar, as depicted in a later stained-glass window in
the Chapel of All Souls College, Oxford.*

The origins of kingship in England can be traced to the second century BC when Celtic and Belgic tribesmen, emigrating from continental Europe, settled in Britain, displacing or absorbing the aboriginal inhabitants (of whom we have no certain knowledge, since we must discount the wonderful fables of Geoffrey of Monmouth told in his *History of the Kings of Britain*). The settlers established a number of tribal kingdoms, stretching as far north as Yorkshire, where the powerful Brigantes (from the area of modern Burgundy) and Parisii (whose name survives in the city of Paris, their original homeland) held sway. Other kingdoms included those of the Iceni in East Anglia, the Catuvellauni further south, the Cantii in modern Kent, the Atrebates and Regni in modern Hampshire and Sussex, the Dumnonii in Cornwall and the Silures on the borders of South Wales. Each of these tribes was ruled by a king (or occasionally a queen) and attained a degree of civilisation that included the minting of coins in gold, silver and copper based on Greek and Roman prototypes and a lively trade with merchants from the Continent.

Stories of the riches of the island of Britain reached the ears of Julius Caesar during his conquest of Gaul and he determined on an expedition to see things for himself. News of his plans crossed the channel before him and the tribes of southern Britain formed a coalition to withstand invasion under the leadership of Cassivellaunus, King of the Catuvellauni, whose capital was near the modern town of Wheathampstead in Hertfordshire. The resistance was so successful that Caesar, after two campaigns in successive years, deemed it prudent to withdraw in September 54 BC.

Cassivellaunus continued to reign peacefully for several years. He moved his capital to Verulamium (St Albans) and was succeeded on his death by his son Andoco, followed by Tasciovanus, the son or brother of Andoco. His son and successor, Cunobelinus ('The Hound of Bel'), who has become Shakespeare's Cymbeline, was a mighty king who moved the capital to Camulodunum (Colchester) and struck a prolific coinage in gold and silver. It was only after his death in about AD 40 that the Romans again contemplated the conquest of Britain. The Roman Emperor Claudius launched his campaign in AD 43 and the conquest was completed in nine years, ending with the capture of Caratacus, son of Cunobelinus and leader of the resistance. The rulers of the other Celtic tribes submitted to Rome and were allowed to continue as 'client kings'. The revolt of Boudicca (popularly known as Boadicea), Queen of the Iceni, in AD 61–2 was the last against Roman rule and was wellnigh successful.

Britain nevertheless became a province of the Roman Empire and remained so for over three hundred years. During this time lines of tribal kings continued to hold sway, their names being preserved in the genealogies passed down orally by bards and first written down several centuries later. It has long been established that oral tradition is often remarkably accurate and free from the embellishments and interpolations that abound in written history.

The Romans withdrew from Britain early in the fifth century when, faced with trouble on the eastern borders of the empire, they needed to muster as many troops as possible. Hadrian's Wall, which had been erected to guard the north of Britain from Pictish and Caledonian incursions, was left unmanned. The British King Vortigern (a title rather than a name), unable to repel the raiders, invited the Jutish mercenaries Hengest and Horsa to help him. He rewarded them with a grant of land, but they later turned against him and drove the Britons out of Kent, establishing the first of the Anglo-Saxon kingdoms there.

In the course of the next century parties of Angles, Saxons and Jutes arrived in vast numbers. Gradually they drove the Britons into Wales and Cornwall and carved out kingdoms for themselves. The stories of the great folk hero, the legendary King Arthur, who led the resistance against the new invaders, belong to this period; but it is almost impossible to disentangle fact from fiction and although Arthur was probably a real person, it is by no means certain that he was a king.

The Anglo-Saxon kingdoms became known as the Heptarchy, 'the rule of seven', but the number of kingdoms varied and there were sometimes more and sometimes less than this number. Although they were quite independent of each other, the kingdoms formed a loosely knit confederation headed by one king, known as the Bretwalda or head king. Seven of these were listed by the Venerable Bede (672–735) in his *History of the English Church and People*, a valuable contemporary source for the early history of Anglo-Saxon England.

The British kings who had been driven out were for the most part Celtic Christians, but the Saxon dynasties were pagan, most lines deriving their descent from Woden, the mythical god-king, renowned in Scandinavian legend as Odin. The pedigrees are recorded in the *Anglo-Saxon Chronicle*. Ethelbert I, King of Kent (d.616), the great-great-grandson of Hengest and third Bretwalda, was the first Anglo-Saxon king to embrace Christianity. He had married a Christian Merovingian princess, Bertha, daughter of Caribert I, King of Paris, and she was allowed to bring her own chaplain to Kent with her and to practise her religion. Ethelbert, therefore, already knew much about the Christian faith when Pope Gregory's mission, headed by St Augustine, landed in 597, and his conversion and baptism were swiftly accomplished. There was a short-lived lapse into paganism under Ethelbert's son and successor Eadbald, chiefly occasioned by the fact that he took his father's young widow to wife, but he was persuaded to put her away and thereafter led an exemplary life. Many Saxon saints and holy abbesses are numbered among his descendants.

The kingdom of the East Saxons, or Essex, was the next to receive the faith under its ruler Saebert (d.616/7), whose mother was Ethelbert's sister, and by the end of the seventh century all the kingdoms of the Heptarchy had become Christian. The kingdoms of East Anglia and Mercia rivalled that of Kent in the piety of their reigning families, whose members founded and endowed many churches and monasteries, while princesses and widowed queens sought solace by entering the religious life.

2. The figure of Ethelbert, King of Kent, from the Chapel of All Souls College, Oxford.

The first of the seven Bretwaldas listed by Bede was Ælla, King of Sussex (fl.477–514), the founder, with his three sons, of the South Saxon kingdom. Their battles are recorded by the *Anglo-Saxon Chronicle*, but strangely their descent and their successors in Sussex are not and Sussex is the kingdom of which least is known. The second Bretwalda was Ceawlin, King of the West Saxons or Wessex (reigned 560–91). His grandfather Cerdic had founded the kingdom in 519, having come to Britain with his son Cynric and five ships in 495. The third Bretwalda was Ethelbert of Kent, already mentioned, and the fourth Redwald, King of East Anglia (died c.617), who was baptised in youth but reverted to paganism and is believed to be the king honoured by the ship burial at Sutton Hoo, near Ipswich, the treasures from which are now in the British Museum. Edwin, King of Northumbria (d.633), was the fifth Bretwalda. He married Ethelburga, the daughter of Ethelbert of Kent, and was converted to Christianity by her chaplain Paulinus about a year later.

In October 633 Edwin was killed in battle with Cadwallon, King of Gwynedd (North Wales), and the pagan Penda, King of Mercia. Queen Ethelburga managed to return to Kent, where she became the first

Abbess of Lyminge, where St Ethelburga's Well and, more prosaically, the Ethelburga Tea-Rooms perpetuate her memory. Edwin was succeeded in the kingdom of Deira (his paternal inheritance) by his cousin Osric, after whose death about a year later Oswald, King of Bernicia, again united the two northern realms into one, Northumbria. He is reckoned as the sixth Bretwalda. He vanquished Cadwallon of Gwynedd in a battle near Hexham in 634, but was himself killed by Penda of Mercia at Oswestry in August 641. He was renowned for his great piety and after feeding a crowd of poor and needy with his own food and breaking up and distributing the silver dish in which it was contained, he was blessed by St Aidan, Bishop of Lindisfarne, who prayed that Oswald's right hand might 'never wither with age'. Bede records that the uncorrupted hand and arm of St Oswald were preserved in a silver casket and venerated at Bamburgh. Presumably the relic disappeared at the Dissolution of the Monasteries. Oswald's brother or half-brother Oswy succeeded him as King of Bernicia and annexed Deira in 654. He succeeded in defeating and killing Penda of Mercia in November 654 and also annexed that kingdom until 657, when it was peacefully restored to Penda's son Wulfhere, who had become a Christian. Oswy is the seventh and last Bretwalda listed by Bede.

His second wife was Eanfled, the daughter of Edwin and Ethelburga, and when he died in February 670, he was succeeded by his and Eanfled's son Egfrith (d.685).

Throughout the next century the dominant kingdoms of the Heptarchy were Wessex and Mercia. An outstanding king of Wessex was Ine (reigned 688–726), who was reclaimed from a life of debauchery by his wife Ethelburga to become a great benefactor of the Church and the promulgator of a code of laws. Finally in 726 he abdicated and went on pilgrimage to Rome, where he died.

Mercia reached its apogee under Offa, who obtained the throne in 757 after defeating and putting to flight his predecessor. In the course of a reign of 39 years he brought almost all England under his sway, adopting the style of *rex totius Anglorum patriae* and being addressed as 'King of the English' by Pope Adrian I. Offa's greatest achievement was the construction of Offa's Dyke, the great earthwork stretching from the Wye to the

3. *The figure of Oswald, King of Northumbria, from the stained-glass windows in the Chapel of All Souls College, Oxford.*

Dee in order to restrain Welsh marauders. He also formulated a code of laws, later adapted by Alfred the Great. It was during Offa's reign that a new wave of Danish pirates began to raid British shores. Offa's Queen Cynethryth was a power to be reckoned with and her name and effigy appear on some of his coins. She was said to have been of foreign origin and it was perhaps her influence that led Offa to follow a continental practice of having their only son Egfrith anointed and crowned king in his father's lifetime in 787. Following Offa's death in July 796, Egfrith succeeded him but only reigned for 141 days, dying childless in December. Thereafter the glory departed from the Mercian kingdom, which passed to a distant kinsman.

Offa had married one of his daughters to King Beohrtric of Wessex in 789. She was named Eadburh (or, more euphoniously, Eadburga) and was destined to gain a reputation rivalling that of her mother. A rival claimant to Wessex was Egbert, who descended from a brother of King Ine and probably had a better claim than Beohrtric, whose exact genealogy is not recorded. Beohrtric, with his father-in-law's support, banished Egbert, who took refuge at the Frankish court of Charlemagne. Queen Eadburh later grew jealous of one of her husband's confidential advisers and prepared a poisoned cup for him to drink from at a banquet. By mistake, the king drank from it instead and died. To escape the consequences of her evil deed Eadburh fled to France, where she presided as the abbess of a convent for a few years and then set out on a pilgrimage to Rome, dying *en route* as a beggar in the streets of Pavia. The people of Wessex had been so horrified by her deed that they decreed that no future royal consort should bear the title of *regina* but be styled *hlafdig* (lady) or *cwen* (companion), whence the word 'queen'. However, this ruling did not obtain for very long.

Portraits *and* Dreſses *of the* KINGS *of* ENGLAND, *with their* Arms *prior to the* Norman Conquest *Plate 4

4. *Alfred's four immediate successors, Edward the Elder, Athelstan, Edmund and Edred, as they appeared to the imagination of an eighteenth-century engraver. The coats of arms are also imaginary.*

It is not clear if Egbert had returned to England before Beohrtric's death, but his succession to the throne was accomplished peacefully and in the course of a reign of 37 years he conquered Kent (to which he had dynastic pretensions) and Mercia, and made himself master of all England south of the Humber. In his latter years he managed to repel Danish invaders who had allied themselves with the Cornish. While in exile Egbert had married Raedburh (Redburga), apparently a niece of one of Charlemagne's wives, and it was their son Ethelwulf who succeeded him in the latter half of 839.

Ethelwulf had served as his father's deputy in Kent, Essex, Sussex and Surrey since 825, so was no stranger to government. Most of his reign was occupied in coping with the Danes, whose raids were made in increasing numbers. Ethelwulf married Osburh, the daughter of his cup-bearer Oslac and a descendant of rulers of the Isle of Wight. She bore him four sons and one daughter. The sons, Ethelbald, Ethelbert, Ethelred and Alfred, all ruled in turn after their father. It was after Osburh's death that Ethelwulf went on pilgrimage to Rome, taking his youngest son, Alfred, with him. On the return journey he stopped at the court of Charles the Bald in France and married that king's daughter Judith, who was crowned queen on her wedding day in October 856. They returned to England and Ethelwulf died a little over a year later on 13 January 858. His eldest son and successor Ethelbald dis-

5. *The figure of Athelstan, grandson of Alfred the Great, from the Chapel of All Souls College, Oxford.*

graced himself by marrying his young stepmother Judith, but was soon persuaded by the Church to repudiate her. She returned to France and in due course married Count Baldwin I of Flanders, becoming the mother of Count Baldwin II, who was to marry Alfred the Great's daughter Elfthryth and become the ancestor of William the Conqueror's Queen Matilda.

Ethelbald was followed by his brothers Ethelbert (reigned 860–65) and Ethelred I (reigned 860–71). The latter spent his whole reign fighting the Danes and eventually died of wounds received in battle with them.

There are, of course, no authentic portraits of these early kings and queens. The coins of some of the Celtic rulers depict crude heads, but they are derived from Roman models and cannot be said to be an attempt at portraiture. Similarly, the coins of the Saxon kings provide only the most grotesque caricatures.

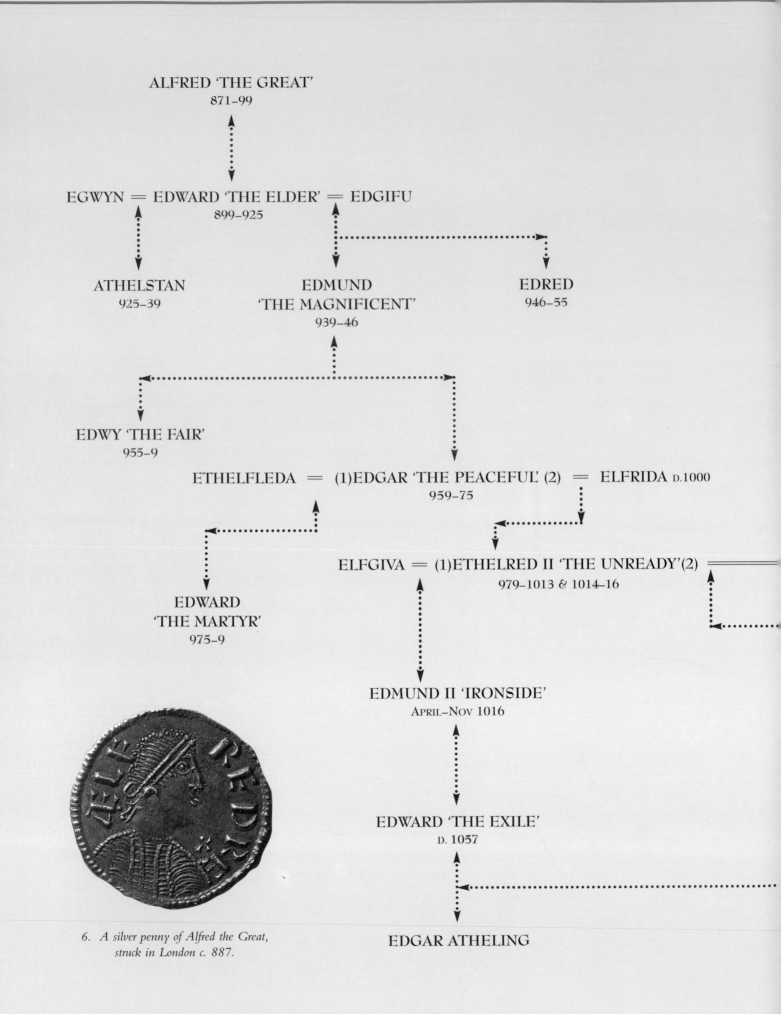

ALFRED 'THE GREAT'
871–99

EGWYN = EDWARD 'THE ELDER' = EDGIFU
899–925

ATHELSTAN
925–39

EDMUND
'THE MAGNIFICENT'
939–46

EDRED
946–55

EDWY 'THE FAIR'
955–9

ETHELFLEDA = (1)EDGAR 'THE PEACEFUL' (2) = ELFRIDA D.1000
959–75

EDWARD
'THE MARTYR'
975–9

ELFGIVA = (1)ETHELRED II 'THE UNREADY'(2) =
979–1013 & 1014–16

EDMUND II 'IRONSIDE'
APRIL–NOV 1016

EDWARD 'THE EXILE'
D. 1057

6. *A silver penny of Alfred the Great,*
struck in London c. 887.

EDGAR ATHELING

THE ANGLO-SAXONS AND DANES

Alfred was born at the Royal Manor of Wantage in Berkshire (now relocated in Oxfordshire) in 849, according to his biographer Asser, but statements of his age at various dates would indicate a year or two earlier. In 853, according to Asser, Alfred was sent to Rome by his father and was there confirmed and invested as a Roman consul by Pope Leo IV, an act elaborated by Asser to be indicative of Alfred's future kingship. Two years later Alfred went to Rome again, accompanying his father King Ethelwulf, and acquiring a stepmother on the return journey.

ALFRED THE GREAT
871–99

Nothing is recorded of Alfred during the reigns of his brothers Ethelbald (858–60) and Ethelbert (860–65), but it seems that it was during those years that he learnt to read and write and became a proficient scholar at a time when few apart from ecclesiastics were literate. His love of learning appears to have been inculcated at an early age by

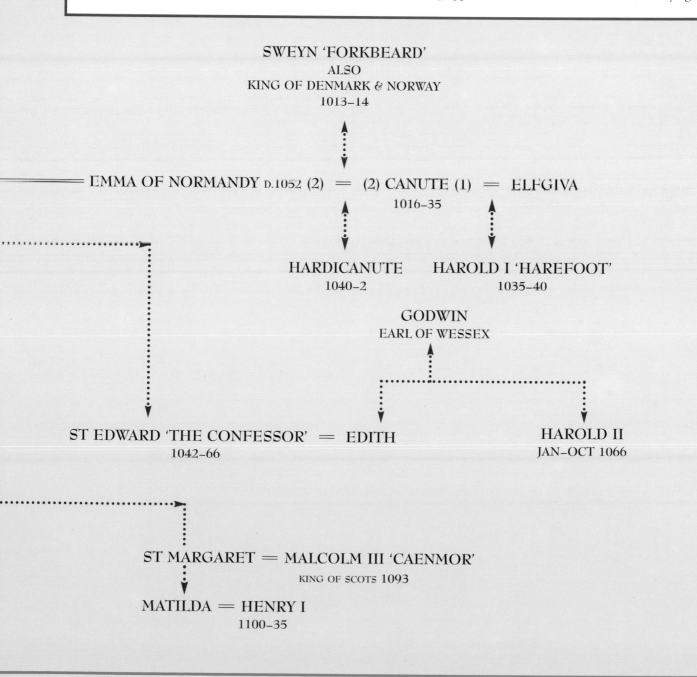

SWEYN 'FORKBEARD'
ALSO
KING OF DENMARK & NORWAY
1013–14

EMMA OF NORMANDY D.1052 (2) = (2) CANUTE (1) = ELFGIVA
1016–35

HARDICANUTE   HAROLD I 'HAREFOOT'
1040–2   1035–40

GODWIN
EARL OF WESSEX

ST EDWARD 'THE CONFESSOR' = EDITH   HAROLD II
1042–66   JAN–OCT 1066

ST MARGARET = MALCOLM III 'CAENMOR'
KING OF SCOTS 1093

MATILDA = HENRY I
1100–35

his mother, Osburh, who promised to give a beautifully illuminated book of Saxon poetry to the first of her sons who could 'recite it' to her. Alfred took the book to his tutor and apparently learnt to recite it parrot fashion, thus winning the prize.

Following the accession of his brother Ethelred in 865, Alfred's position became increasingly important. He served as second-in-command in the wars with the Danish invaders and was generally regarded as heir presumptive. In 868 he married Ealhswith, daughter of Ethelred Mucil, Ealdorman of the Gaini (a tribal division of Mercia) and his wife Eadburh, a descendant of the Mercian royal family. In the year of his marriage Alfred suffered a mysterious illness which was to recur periodically throughout his life. It has been suggested that this may have been an early manifestation of porphyria, 'the royal malady', that was to afflict many of Alfred's descendants, most notably George III.

When King Ethelred died of battle wounds in April 871, his two sons were still young children, and it was Alfred who became his successor and was probably crowned or consecrated as king at either Winchester or Kingston upon Thames, where the ancient coronation stone of the West Saxon kings, which gave the town its name, still stands.

The first five years of Alfred's reign were spent in indecisive battles with the Danes, who withdrew to Mercia in 877, after forcing Alfred to retire for the winter to the marshy island of Athelney in Somerset. Alfred is said to have journeyed to the Danish camp disguised as a wandering minstrel to spy out the strength of his enemy and gain some knowledge of their plans. From this period also comes the apocryphal story (interpolated into Asser's account by Matthew Parker, Archbishop of Canterbury in the reign of Elizabeth I) of Alfred seeking shelter in a herdsman's cottage and being soundly berated by the herdsman's wife for allowing the cakes she had set him to watch burn, as he pondered on his problems.

In the spring of 878 Alfred and his army emerged from Athelney and after gathering large contingents on the way, met the Danish army at Ethandune (Edington), where they gained a great victory. A peace treaty was concluded soon after and the Danes retreated into East Anglia, Mercia and Northumbria, which were ceded to them and renamed the Danelaw.

Alfred spent the rest of his reign consolidating his kingdom, strengthening his army, founding a navy, and above all encouraging learning and religion throughout his realm. He died in London on 26 October 899 and was buried in the New Minster (later Hyde Abbey) at Winchester. His wife Ealhswith died on 5 December 902. They had five surviving children: Ethelfleda, 'Lady of the Mercians', who married Ethelred, Ealdorman of Mercia, and warred with the Danes and the Welsh; Edward, who succeeded his father; Ethelgiva, Abbess of Shaftesbury; Elfthryth, who married Baldwin II, Count of Flanders, as already mentioned; and Ethelweard, who died in 922.

EDWARD 'THE ELDER'
899–925

The elder son of Alfred was probably born in 871 or 872. He was crowned at Kingston upon Thames on 8 June 900. His accession was contested by his cousin Ethelwold, the son of King Ethelred, who had been passed over as a child in favour of Alfred. Edward soon chased him out and he sought refuge in the Danelaw, whence he continued to make raids until he was finally defeated and killed in 904.

In the course of his reign Edward regained territory south of the Humber from the Danelaw and was acknowledged as overlord by the Danish king of York, the king of Scots, the king of Strathclyde and other minor rulers.

Edward is noteworthy for having married three times and being the father of a large family. His first wife, Ecgwynn (Egwina), is said on no very good authority to have been 'of humble origin'. She was the mother of his successor Athelstan and of a daughter. Edward's second wife was Elfleda, daughter of Ealdorman Ethelhelm. She bore him two sons who died young and unmarried, and six daughters, four of whom made grand continental marriages arranged by their half-brother Athelstan, and two of whom became nuns. Edward the Elder's third wife was Eadgifu, daughter of Ealdorman Sigehelm of Kent. She became the mother of Edmund and Edred, both subsequently kings, and two daughters.

Edward the Elder died at Farndon-on-Dee in Mercia on 17 July 925 and was buried at Winchester. His widow Eadgifu survived him for many years, dying in the reign of her grandson King Edgar on 25 August 968.

7. *An eighteenth-century imaginary portrait of four Anglo-Saxon kings, striking dramatic poses,*
including (for good measure) Olaf Tryggvesson of Norway.

ATHELSTAN
925–39

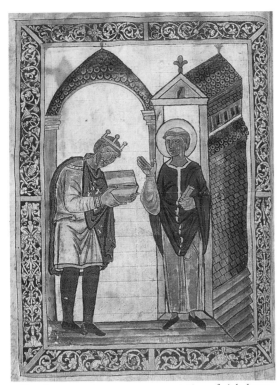

8. A near-contemporary representation of Athelstan presenting a book to St Cuthbert, from a manuscript version of Bede's Life of St Cuthbert *made c.930.*

Athelstan was born in about 895 and as a small child was a great favourite with his grandfather, King Alfred. He was about 30 years old when he succeeded his father and was crowned at Kingston upon Thames on 5 September 925. Within two years he had expelled the Viking Guthfrith from the kingdom of York and also received the submission of Constantine II, King of Scots, and a Welsh king. He invaded Scotland in 933, when he 'harried much of the country' and in 937 won a great victory over the Danes at Brunanburh near the Humber, killing, it is claimed, five kings and eight chieftains. This left Athelstan the acknowledged overlord of all Britain and he settled down to formulating laws, including one forbidding Sunday trading and another decreeing that perjurers might not be buried in consecrated ground.

Athelstan forged a strong foreign policy by marrying his many half-sisters to continental rulers, including Charles the Simple, King of France, Hugh the Great, Duke of France and Count of Paris, and the Emperor Otto I. Shortly before his death he despatched a fleet to Flanders to aid his nephew Louis IV to regain the French throne, initiating the first involvement of English forces in Europe.

Athelstan died at Gloucester on 27 October 939 and was buried at Malmesbury Abbey, which he had founded. He never married and was succeeded by his half-brother Edmund.

EDMUND 'THE MAGNIFICENT'
939–46

Edmund, the son of Edward the Elder and his third wife Eadgifu, was born about 921. He was about 18 when he succeeded Athelstan and was crowned at Kingston upon Thames on 16 October 939. Edmund was as energetic and warlike as his predecessors and wrested many towns from the Danes, including Leicester, Lincoln, Nottingham, Derby and Stamford. He subdued Northumbria and Strathclyde, which he ceded to Malcolm I, King of Scots, in order to assure the latter's allegiance.

Edmund was dining with his entourage at Pucklechurch in Gloucestershire on 26 May 946 when an outlaw named Liofa was spotted as an intruder. The king took part in the struggle to arrest him and received a fatal stab wound in the stomach, dying almost immediately. He was only 25 and was buried at Glastonbury Abbey.

Edmund had married at about the time of his accession Elfgifu (Elfgiva), who was regarded as a Saxon saint. She bore him two sons and died soon after the birth of the younger in 944, being buried at Shaftesbury. Edmund then married Ethelfleda of Damerham, daughter of Ealdorman Alfgar. There were no children of the marriage and Ethelfleda later married Ealdorman Athelstan. She was still living in 975. Edmund's sons, Edwy and Edgar, were both small children when he died and he was succeeded by his brother Edred.

EDRED
946–55

Edred, the youngest son of Edward the Elder, was born about 923. He was crowned at Kingston upon Thames on 16 August 946, and bravely continued Edmund's work, although afflicted from birth with an unspecified physical disability that precluded him from marriage. He died at Frome, Somerset, on 23 November 955, aged about 32, and was buried at Winchester. He was succeeded by his nephew Edwy, the elder son of Edmund.

EDWY
955–9

9. An imaginary portrait of King Edred
from an eighteenth-century engraving.

Edwy was born about 941 and at 14 was considered old enough to rule under the tutelage of Oda, Archbishop of Canterbury, and Dunstan, Abbot of Glastonbury. His coronation at Kingston upon Thames took place in January 956. The young king had married secretly (or at least pledged himself to marry) his kinswoman Elfgifu. Their exact relationship is not known, but her mother, Ethelgifu, may have been a sister of the king's mother. Edwy found the long feasting following the corona- tion tedious and slipped away to

10. A similar imaginary portrait
of King Edwy.

enjoy the company of his beloved and her mother. Archbishop Oda noticed his absence and sent Dunstan to find him. The latter, horrified to discover that Edwy had contracted an alliance within the prohibited degrees of kinship, upbraid- ed and even physically attacked the two women, dragging the unwilling king back to the banquet. Edwy retaliated by exiling Dunstan, but in 958 Oda declared his marriage or betrothal invalid. Elfgifu died at Gloucester in suspicious cir- cumstances in September 959 and Edwy followed her on 1 October 959. The two untimely deaths were certainly brought about by the open hostility of Oda and Dunstan towards the young king. Dunstan's star was in the ascendant. He succeeded Oda as Archbishop of Canterbury in 961 and reached the height of his power and influence under Edwy's brother and successor Edgar.

EDGAR 'THE PEACEFUL'
959–75

Edgar was born in 943 or 944 and had been associated in the government with Edwy since 957, Mercia and the Danelaw being placed under his jurisdiction. On becoming sole ruler in 959 he was guided completely by Dunstan, who became virtually the chief minister. Edgar's overlordship was accepted by all the other rulers in Britain: the North Welsh princes agreed to pay a tribute of 300 wolves' heads annually for four years; the goodwill of the Scots was secured by the cession of Lothian; and a limited autonomy was allowed to the Danes in the north.

Edgar married Ethelfleda, daughter of Ealdorman Ordmaer in 961 and she apparently died in childbirth the fol- lowing year, leaving one son, Edward. Edgar did not remarry immediately but formed a strong attachment to a girl named Wulfthrith (Wulfrida), who is said to have been a nun (probably a lay sister). She gave birth to a daughter, Eadgyth (or Edith), at Kemsing in Kent, and shortly thereafter took the child to the nunnery at Wilton, near Salisbury, where both were to remain for the rest of their lives. Eadgyth gained a great reputation for sanctity, refused the office of abbess, and after her death was venerated as a saint. Edgar married a second time in 964, his new wife being Elfthrith (Elfrida), daughter of Ordgar, Ealdorman of Devon, and widow of Edgar's friend Ethelwold, Ealdorman of East Anglia. She was a woman of strong character and was destined to make her mark in history.

It is presumed that Edgar had been crowned at Kingston upon Thames soon after his accession in accordance with custom, but some fourteen years later Dunstan planned a much grander ceremony, based on the coronation rite of the Frankish kings. The Order he drew up has remained the basis of all subsequent coronations. Edgar and Elfrida were solemnly crowned and anointed at Bath Abbey on Whit Sunday, 11 May 973. Elfrida was the first king's wife to be acknowledged in this way since King Ethelwulf's second wife Judith had been crowned on her wedding day over a hundred years previously.

11. A contemporary portrait of King Edgar from his Charter to the New Minster at Winchester, dated 966. He is shown flanked by the Virgin Mary and St Peter, adoring Christ in Majesty.

After the coronation Edgar went to Chester, where he received the homage of six (or eight, according to some) subject kings, who, in token of their submission, rowed him in state on the River Dee from his palace to the monastery of St John the Baptist and back. Edgar only survived another two years, dying on 8 July 975, aged about 31 or 32. He was buried beside his father at Glastonbury. Elfrida, who was to survive him for many years, had borne him two sons: Edmund, who died young in 971; and Ethelred, who was to succeed his half-brother Edward as king.

EDWARD 'THE MARTYR'
975–9

The only son of Edgar by his first wife was born about 962 and was consequently 13 when he succeeded his father. He was crowned by Dunstan at Kingston upon Thames within days of his accession, probably because his stepmother Elfrida claimed that her son Ethelred, as the son of parents who had both been crowned, had a better right to the throne, a view in keeping with the thought of the time. Elfrida and Ethelred lived at Corfe Castle in Dorset and

12. *An eighteenth-century engraving of the murder of Edward the Martyr at Corfe Castle.*

the unsuspecting Edward called upon them in the course of a hunting trip on 18 March 979. His stepmother handed him a stirrup cup and as he raised it to his lips her servants attacked him, stabbing him in the back. His horse bolted and he was dragged along the ground with his foot caught in a stirrup, receiving multiple injuries from which he soon died. He was buried at Wareham 'with no royal honours', but within a few years miracles began to be attributed to his intercession and he was exhumed and reinterred at Shaftesbury. His alleged bones were found there in the course of an archaeological dig in 1931 and a long dispute ensued regarding their final disposal. They eventually found rest in the Russian Orthodox chapel of St Edward at Brookwood Cemetery, Surrey, in December 1988. Edward was not married and was succeeded by his half-brother Ethelred.

ETHELRED 'THE UNREADY'
979–1013 and 1014–16

Ethelred, the younger but only surviving son of King Edgar and Elfrida, was born about 968 and was therefore a boy of 10 or 11 when he witnessed the murder of his half-brother in March 979, and could hardly have been implicated in the crime. His accession was accepted as he was the only heir and Dunstan crowned him at Kingston upon Thames on 14 April 979. Elfrida deemed it prudent to retire to the Benedictine priory she had founded at Wherwell in Hampshire and pass the rest of her life there as a nun. She died on 17 November 1000.

Ethelred's nickname 'the Unready', although apt, is an incorrect rendering of the original 'Redeless', signifying lacking in counsel. His reign was beset by pirate raids, a pestilence among cattle (an early appearance of foot and mouth disease, no doubt), and in 994 a raid by the Norwegian King Olaf Tryggvesson and the Danish King Sweyn 'Forkbeard', who sailed up the Thames with 94 ships and besieged London until the king and his council bought them off for £16,000, initiating a policy of paying regular protection money which became known as *Danegeld*.

An uneasy peace was maintained for several years until, on St Brice's Day (13 November) 1003, Ethelred suddenly ordered the murder of all Danes living in England. Among them was Sweyn of Denmark's sister. He renewed his attack in 1004, sacking and burning Norwich. A famine the following year forced the Danes to withdraw, but they soon returned and in the course of the next few years brought the whole of England under their rule. Sweyn was acknowledged as king in 1013 and Ethelred fled to the Isle of Wight and thence to Normandy. He was recalled on Sweyn's death the following year and ruled uneasily until his death in London on 23 April 1016. He was buried in St Paul's Cathedral.

Ethelred was married first in about 985 to Elfgiva, daughter of Thored, Ealdorman of Northumbria. She became the mother of many sons and daughters, some of whom died before their father. Elfgiva died in 1000 or 1001 and in April 1002 Ethelred married Emma, the eldest daughter of Duke Richard I of Normandy. She adopted the popular English name of Elfgifu (Elfgiva), and in due time gave birth to Alfred, Edward and Godgifu. Emma was to have an eventful life. Ethelred was succeeded by Edmund 'Ironside', the eldest surviving son of his first marriage.

13. *Ethelred the Unready brandishing an outsize sword, from the* Chronicle of Abingdon *of c.1220.*

SWEYN 'FORKBEARD'
1013–14

Sweyn, the son of Harald Bluetooth, King of Denmark, probably by his second wife Tove, daughter of Mistivoj, Prince of the Wends, was born about 970 and succeeded his father as King of Denmark in 986. The story of his raids and final conquest of England has already been related. He only held his conquered kingdom for six months as he died at Gainsborough following a fall from his horse on 3 February 1014. His body was returned to Denmark and buried in Roskilde Cathedral.

Sweyn's first wife was Gunhild, daughter of Mieszko I, Duke of Poland and his first wife Dubravka, daughter of Boleslav I, Duke of Bohemia. She became the mother of Harald IV, King of Denmark and Canute, who was destined to become the ruler of a vast Scandinavian empire. Sweyn's second wife was a formidable lady named Sigrid the Haughty, the divorced wife of King Eric the Victorious of Sweden. Her daughter by Sweyn was destined to become the ancestor of later sovereigns of Denmark.

14. An engraved portrait of Sweyn, after an image on a contemporary Danish coin.

EDMUND 'IRONSIDE'
1016

Edmund was the third son of Ethelred the Unready and his first wife Elfgiva and was born about 993. His two elder brothers, Athelstan and Egbert, both predeceased their father and on Ethelred's death in April 1016 Edmund was chosen as King by 'all the councillors who were in London and the citizens'. He was crowned at St Paul's Cathedral almost immediately.

15. Canute and Elfgiva/Emma presenting an altar cross to the New Minster at Winchester, from the Liber Vitae *of 1031.*

Edmund, nicknamed 'Ironside' on account of his great courage, at once found his position contested by Sweyn's son Canute. A fierce battle was fought at Ashingdon in Essex and Canute won the day, but the two met at Alney in Gloucestershire after the battle and agreed on a division of the kingdom, whereby Edmund took Wessex and Canute Mercia. The arrangement did not last for long as Edmund died at Oxford on 30 November 1016, murdered according to a later legend by the son of one of his enemies, who stabbed him in a privy. He was buried at Glastonbury.

Edmund was married in the summer of 1015 to Ealdgith, widow of Sigeferth, son of Earngrim, an Anglo-Scandinavian. Edmund and Edward, the two (possibly twin) sons she bore him, were sent to Hungary for safe-keeping.

CANUTE
1016–35

Canute was born in Denmark about 995 and as a youth and young man accompanied his father Sweyn on his English expeditions. After his father's death he was chosen king by the Danish fleet but failed to establish his position until his victory at Ashingdon and his agreement to divide the kingdom with Edmund Ironside. On Edmund's death he became the undisputed ruler of all England and was crowned at St Paul's Cathedral on 6 January 1017. Two years later he succeeded his elder brother Harald as king of Denmark. In 1030 Canute conquered Norway and became the master of a vast Scandinavian empire. He secured his position by a series of assassinations, including that of Edwy, the last surviving son of Ethelred the

Unready's first marriage, and would have killed **Edmund Ironside's** sons also, had they not been taken to Hungary. There was another side to Canute's character, too, and he subsidised the tolls of pilgrims to Rome, codified English laws, and in a well-known story rebuked his flattering courtiers who had told him he could turn the tide at his command. To demonstrate the untruth of this he had his chair set by the seashore and when the incoming tide had covered his feet told his followers to observe 'how empty and worthless is the power of kings'. He is said to have followed this by removing his crown and setting it on the head of a figure of Christ on the cross.

In his early youth Canute contracted a 'handfast' marriage in the Danish manner (a union unblessed by the church) with Elfgiva, daughter of Elfhelm, Ealdorman of Northampton, and they had two sons, Sweyn and Harold. After his coronation, however, he repudiated her in order to make a grander alliance. He sent to Normandy for Ethelred's widow Emma, who must have been his senior by some ten years. She returned with alacrity and was married to him on 2 July 1017, thus becoming queen a second time. They had a son, Hardicanute, later king, and a daughter, Gunhild, who (renamed Kunigunde) became the first wife of the Emperor Henry III.

Canute died at Shaftesbury on 12 November 1035, aged no more than 40, and was buried at Winchester, where the painted wooden chests containing the mingled bones of Saxon and Danish kings may still be seen on top of the cathedral choir screen. Canute's coins depict him as a helmeted figure, as befits a warrior king.

HAROLD 'HAREFOOT'
1035–40

Harold, nicknamed 'Harefoot' from his prowess as a runner, was born about 1016, the younger son of Canute and Elfgiva of Northampton. In 1030 his mother, a very able woman, and his elder brother Sweyn were sent by Canute to govern the newly conquered Norway on his behalf, but Harold remained in England. On his father's death he was chosen by the Council to be co-ruler with his half-brother Hardicanute, who was absent in Denmark. Two years later Hardicanute was still absent and Harold was recognised as sole king and crowned at Oxford. His first act was to banish his stepmother, Emma, who went to Bruges. After an uneventful reign Harold died at Oxford on 17 March 1040, aged about 24. His body was brought to London and buried at St Clement Danes, but Hardicanute later had it disinterred, beheaded and flung into the marshes that bordered the Thames. Harold never married, but there is some evidence that he had a mistress, yet another Elfgifu or Elfgiva, who bore him a son, Aelfwine, the founder of a monastery in Aquitaine in 1060.

HARDICANUTE
1040–2

Hardicanute, the son of Canute and Emma, was born in England in about 1018. At the age of 10 he accompanied his father to Denmark and was made king there. On Canute's death in 1035, Hardicanute was reluctant to return to England, although regarded as the legitimate successor, and was content to allow his half-brother Harold to assume power.

In 1039 Hardicanute left Denmark and joined his mother in her exile in Bruges. Learning of Harold's death in the following year, he set out with a fleet of 60 ships to claim his kingdom. He landed at Sandwich and proceeded to Canterbury, where he was crowned on 18 June 1040. Hardicanute imposed crippling taxes and in the words of the *Anglo-Saxon Chronicle* 'never did anything worthy of a king'. He did not marry and died in a drunken fit at a wedding feast at Lambeth on 8 June 1042, being buried at Winchester.

EDWARD 'THE CONFESSOR'
1042–66

Edward, the youngest son of Ethelred the Unready and his second wife Emma of Normandy, was born at Islip, Oxfordshire, about 1004. He spent most of his early life in Normandy and only returned to England after his younger half-brother Hardicanute became king there in 1040.

Edward owed his peaceful succession to the throne on Hardicanute's death in 1042 to Godwin, Earl of Wessex, who had risen to a position of great power under Canute and was the virtual ruler of the realm. The new king was crowned

16. The great seal of Edward the Confessor, showing the crowned king enthroned, holding a sword in his left hand and the sceptre with the dove in his right.

at Winchester Cathedral on Easter Sunday, 3 April 1043. He was of a deeply religious turn of mind, more suited to be a priest than a king, and his sobriquet 'the Confessor' indicated that he was one who was prepared to suffer martyrdom for the faith, although he was never actually called upon to do so.

Earl Godwin consolidated his power by marrying Edward to his daughter Edith on 23 January 1045, but the marriage remained unconsummated as Edward had taken a vow of chastity. Nevertheless, Edith was treated with great respect and accorded her own coronation as queen consort. There was a short period in 1051 when Godwin and his family fell out of favour and Queen Edith was sent to a nunnery, but things were soon patched up. The break, however, was to have far-reaching consequences as it induced Edward to promise the succession to his kinsman William, Duke of Normandy, the grandnephew of Edward's mother Emma.

Earl Godwin died in 1053 and his place as the king's chief adviser was taken by his son Harold. Edward had long vowed to make a pilgrimage to Rome, but when it became apparent that affairs of state and increasing infirmity would not permit him to do so, he determined to expiate the vow by building and endowing a magnificent abbey on the Isle of Thorney beside the Thames. The result was Westminster Abbey, destined to become the coronation church as well as the burial place of many of Edward's successors. It was consecrated on Holy Innocents' Day, 28 December 1065, but Edward was too infirm and fevered to attend. He died on 5 January 1066 and was buried in the new foundation, where his shrine still stands. He was canonised by Pope Alexander III in 1161. Queen Edith lived quietly at Winchester until her death on 18 December 1075. William the Conqueror treated her with great respect and had her buried beside Edward.

The Bayeux Tapestry, Edward's coins and his great seal all depict him as a venerable, bearded figure and must be accepted as the nearest contemporary likenesses of the saintly king. He was the first English sovereign to be credited with the healing power of the royal touch, which was claimed and exercised by many of his successors.

HAROLD II
1066

Harold, the second son of Godwin, Earl of Wessex, was born about 1022. His mother Gytha had close connections with the Swedish and Danish royal families and was a kinswoman of King Canute. Harold rose to prominence in the reign of Edward the Confessor, his brother-in-law, and was associated with his father, Earl Godwin, in many of his enterprises. In 1053 he succeeded to the earldom of Wessex and in the course of the next few years greatly increased his land holdings. Harold determined on the subjugation of Gruffydd ap Llywelyn, the powerful Welsh king, and drove him out of Rhuddlan. Gruffydd was killed by his own men and his head was sent to Harold in August 1063. Harold set out to return from Wales by sea and was shipwrecked on the French coast. His captor, Count Guy of Ponthieu, sent him to the court of William of Normandy, who feasted him, betrothed him to one of his young daughters, and by dint of trickery extracted an oath from him that he would support William's claim to England on the death of Edward.

Harold returned home and, disregarding his betrothal to the infant Norman princess, married for political reasons Ealdgyth, the widow of Gruffydd ap Llywelyn and daughter of another former enemy, Earl Aelfgar of East Anglia. Prior to this he had lived in 'handfast' marriage for many years with Eadgyth Swanneshals ('Edith Swan-neck'), a girl from Norfolk, who had borne him a large family of sons and daughters.

On Edward the Confessor's death in January 1066 Harold was at once elected king by the nobles, although possessing no hereditary claim to the throne, and he was crowned in Westminster Abbey immediately after Edward's burial there on 6 January 1066. In April Harold had to cope with marauding raids on the south coast made by his exiled brother Tostig, who managed to elude his clutches and sail away to Scotland. The threat of invasion by William of Normandy was ever present and Harold remained on the Isle of Wight with his army until their provisions ran out in September, when he disbanded his men and returned to London. He soon received news that Harald Hardrada, King of Norway, had landed in the north and been joined by Tostig. In an attempt to win Tostig over to his side, Harold offered him a third of the kingdom, while to the Norwegian king he offered only 'six feet of ground'. The offer was contemptuously refused and Harold was compelled to reassemble his army and march northwards with the utmost speed. He finally encountered the Norwegian force at Stamford Bridge, north of York, and on 25 September inflicted a crushing defeat on them in the course of which both Harald Hardrada and Tostig were slain. He concluded a peace treaty with the Norwegian king's son Olaf and the remnants of the Norwegian fleet were allowed to sail away.

Harold received no respite as news soon arrived that William of Normandy had landed at Hastings on 29 September. There was nothing for it but to rally his exhausted army and commence to march south again, gathering what reinforcements he could on the way. They reached Senlac, near Hastings, and were in the process of fortifying their position when the Normans struck on 14 October. The battle was fiercely fought with great losses on both sides, but the Normans finally won the day by the stratagem of a pretended flight. Harold and two of his brothers, Gurth and Leofwine, were killed. Tradition had it that Harold's eye was pierced by an arrow, but careful examination of the near contemporary Bayeux Tapestry makes it clear that he was cut down by a sword blow and that it was a nearby figure who got the arrow in the eye. William ordered Harold's body to be buried on the sea shore, but a strong tradition relates that his erstwhile mistress Edith Swan-neck was allowed to exhume it and take it for burial to Waltham Abbey in Essex, which Harold had founded in 1060.

His widow Ealdgyth is said to have given birth posthumously to a son, named Harold after his father. She later entered a convent and the date of her death is unknown, although she is said to have been buried at Bishop's Stortford in Hertfordshire. Her son is alleged to have been still living in 1098. Edith Swan-neck's children survived the Conquest and went to live on the Continent. One daughter, Gytha, ended up in Russia, where she married Vladimir Monomakh, Great Prince of Kiev. Nearly 300 years later Harold's blood returned to the throne of England in the persons of Edward III and his queen Philippa, both of whom descended from Gytha.

17.   A silver penny of Harold II struck in 1066, one of
three varieties struck in his short reign.

THE NORMANS

ROBERT II 'THE DEVIL'
DUKE OF NORMANDY

WILLIAM I 'THE CONQUEROR'
DUKE OF NORMANDY
1066–87

WILLIAM II 'RUFUS'
1087–1100

HENRY I = MATILDA
1100–35

ADELA

STEPHEN
1135–54

GEOFFREY V = MATILDA
PLANTAGENET
COUNT OF
ANJOU & MAINE

HENRY II
1154–89

Stephen

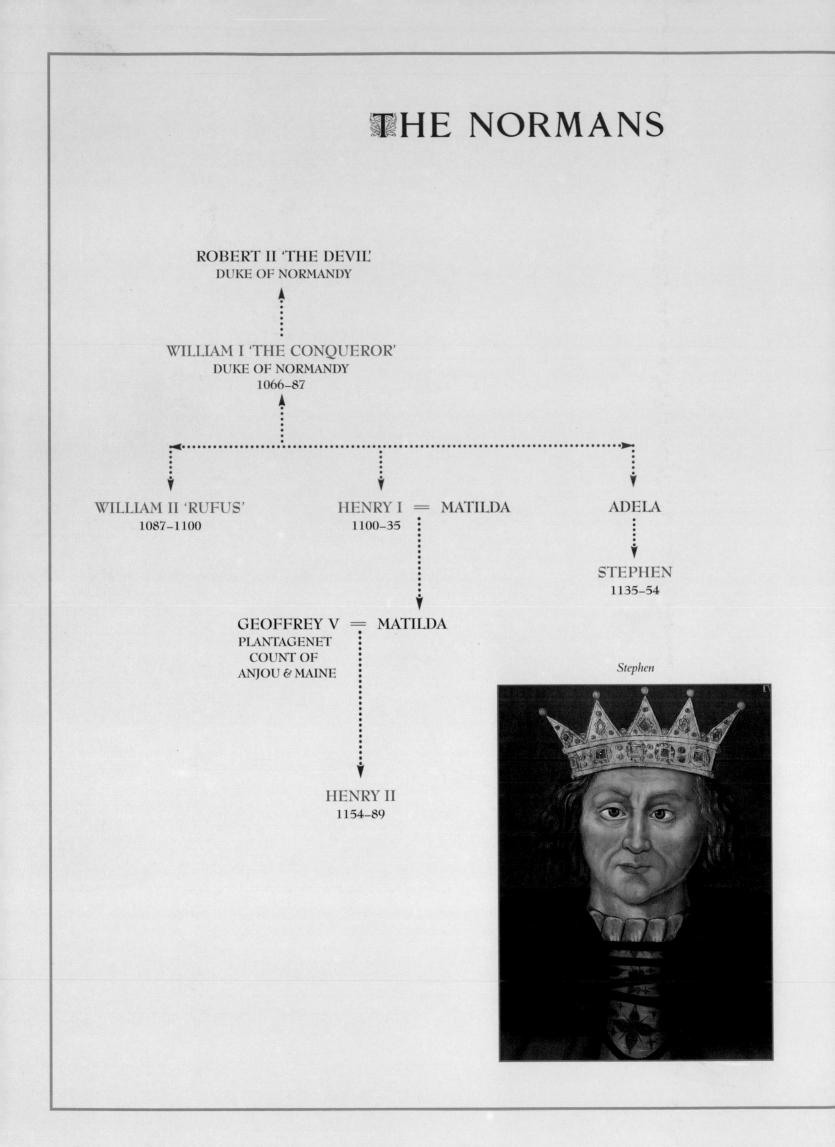

WILLIAM THE CONQUEROR
1066–87

William the Conqueror began life as William the Bastard. He was born at the castle of Falaise in Normandy in 1027, the natural son of Robert the Devil (also called the Magnificent), Duke of Normandy, by a girl of humble origin named Herleve, whose father Fulbert was a local tradesman. It has often been said that the taint of bastardy had a great psychological effect upon William, but it was practically the norm in the ducal house of Normandy and William's father and uncle were the first dukes of their line actually born in lawful wedlock, so it is not very likely that William was conscious of any stigma.

Duke Robert died in 1035 and William succeeded to the duchy at the age of seven or eight, reigning under the protection of three guardians, all of whom fell victim to assassins. An attempt to wrest the duchy from him by his cousin Count Guy of Burgundy and a faction of malcontents was defeated by William while still under 20 years old.

In 1051 William visited his kinsman Edward the Confessor and it was probably during his sojourn at the English court that the idea of succeeding Edward first occurred to him. Indeed, the king himself may have suggested it. On his return to Normandy, William began his court-ship of Matilda, the diminutive daughter of his neighbour Count Baldwin V of Flanders, perhaps motivated in part by knowledge of her descent from Alfred the Great. She rejected his suit at first, but eventually gave in and they were married in 1053. However, there was some ecclesiastical objection to the marriage, the exact nature of which has never been discovered, and it was not until 1059 that the Pope granted a dispensation and the couple were charged to expiate their 'sin' by founding two abbeys at Caen – the Abbaye-aux-Hommes (St Stephen's) and the Abbaye-aux-Dames (Holy Trinity) William and Matilda were an exemplary married couple and became the parents of four sons and six daughters. The story of William extracting an oath from Harold to support his claim to the English crown on the death of Edward has already been told, as has its aftermath. After his victory at Hastings, William marched to London, overcoming all local resistance on the way, and was crowned king at Westminster Abbey on Christmas Day 1066. The coronation was the occasion of a riot when the shouts of acclamation within the abbey alarmed the Norman soldiers on guard outside and they fired houses and killed numerous Saxons before the new king appeared in the abbey doorway to restore order.

18. A silver penny of William the Conqueror, 1068.

It was not until 1071 that the country was sufficiently subdued to allow William to return to Normandy for any length of time. He was a man of prodigious energy, a builder of castles (including the Tower of London), and the architect of the feudal system in England. It was at his command that the Domesday Book was compiled in 1086 to record the names of all landowners and tenants.

William was stern and just and must be regarded as a great ruler and legislator, far in advance of his times. His coins and the representation of him in the Bayeux tapestry show him to have been clean-shaven with a pudding-basin haircut. By tradition he was tall and had a ruddy complexion.

Queen Matilda died at Caen on 2 November 1083 and was buried in the abbey she had founded there. Her eldest son, Robert, gave his father much trouble, although he had been designated heir to the duchy of Normandy. The second son, Richard, was killed while hunting in the New Forest in about 1081, and the third son, his father's favourite and namesake, was destined to succeed to the throne of England.

19. Matilda of Flanders, William the Conqueror's diminutive queen. A drawing based on contemporary descriptions.

In 1087 William was in Normandy striving to maintain his borders from the continual threats of his neighbours the King of France and the Count of Anjou, supported by his son Robert. William had become excessively corpulent and the French King made jokes at his expense, enquiring when he expected to lie in. William rose to the bait, threatening to 'set all France ablaze' on the day of his 'uprising'. In the late summer of 1087 the French garrison at Mantes raided the Norman border and in retaliation William sacked and fired the town. In the course of the action his horse stumbled on a hot cinder and William was flung violently against the high pommel of his saddle, sustaining severe internal injuries. He was taken to the priory of St Gervais, near Rouen, and died there some days later on 8 or 9 September 1087. He was buried in his foundation of St Stephen at Caen.

WILLIAM II 'RUFUS'
1087–1100

William Rufus, so-called from his fierce red hair and ruddy complexion, was born in Normandy between 1056 and 1060, the third son of William the Conqueror. He was his father's favourite son, probably because he bore a close physical resemblance to him, and was designated as heir to the throne of England. The younger William lost no time in consolidating his position on his father's death and was crowned at Westminster Abbey on 26 September 1087.

WILLIAM IIᴰ

Although Rufus possessed some qualities of leadership and was a good soldier, his reputation has suffered at the hands of the Church, which disapproved of his lifestyle and his delaying the appointments of bishops and abbots in order to appropriate the Church revenues for his own use. His debaucheries were described as 'hateful to God and man' and the chronicler William of Malmesbury reported that at William's court it was usual for young men to 'rival women in delicacy of person, to mince their gait, to walk with loose gestures and half naked'. The implication is obvious and is further confirmed by the facts that William never married or was known to have had a mistress.

After his accession, Rufus spent several years campaigning in

20. An eighteenth-century engraving of William Rufus. The likeness is drawn from contemporary descriptions and from coins.

Normandy both for and against his brother Robert. Since England and Normandy were under separate rule, the barons who held lands in both found it very difficult to serve two masters and the problem was temporarily solved in 1096 when Robert joined the First Crusade, pledging Normandy to William for 10,000 marks in order to finance his expedition.

William rendered himself particularly unpopular by his opposition to Archbishop Anselm of Canterbury's attempts to effect reforms in the Church, forcing him to leave the country and appropriating the revenues of the archbishopric.

Rufus met his end on 2 August 1100 on a hunting expedition in the New Forest. According to most accounts, he went in pursuit of a stag, followed by Walter Tirel, one of his knights. The king loosed an arrow but missed the quarry and called out to Tirel to shoot, which he did, accidentally killing Rufus. William was so unpopular that it was left to a handful of peasants to load his body on to a farm cart and take it to Winchester for burial in the cathedral, where the clergy declined to perform any religious rites over it.

William's one creditable action was his rebuilding of the Palace of Westminster, and Westminster Hall was completed in his lifetime. His proud boast was that it was 'but a bedchamber' to the palace he intended to build.

HENRY I
1100–1135

Henry was the youngest son and probably the youngest child of William the Conqueror and Queen Matilda. He was born at Selby in Yorkshire in September or October 1068, his mother having accompanied her husband on his campaign to subdue the north. Henry was his mother's favourite and on her death in 1083 she left him her English estates, which he was not allowed to hold during his father's lifetime. He received a good education, learning to read and write Latin and studying English law, and it would be reasonable to assume that a career in the Church was envisaged for him, as with two elder brothers living the likelihood of his accession to either England or Normandy seemed remote.

After his father's death in 1087, Henry was constantly compelled to switch his allegiance between Robert and William until Robert's cession of Normandy to Rufus in 1096. Henry was one of the hunting party in the New Forest when William met his death and was acknowledged as king by such councillors as were present at Winchester. After hastily securing the treasury, he set out for London and was crowned at Westminster Abbey on 6 August 1100. He then issued a charter promising a return to his father's ways and restored Anselm to the archbishopric of Canterbury.

On 11 November 1100 Henry was married at Westminster Abbey to Edith (renamed Matilda in honour of his mother), the elder daughter of Malcolm III, King of Scots, and St Margaret, the granddaughter of Edmund Ironside, thus reinforcing the strain of Saxon royal blood in the family.

The question of lay investiture of ecclesiastical estates became a difficult issue for several years. Anselm claimed that he held his estates from the Pope and refused to do homage to the king for them. As a result he was again exiled. A compromise was finally reached in 1107 when Henry's sister Adela, Countess of Blois, suggested that the bishops should pay homage for fiefs held of the king, who in his turn would allow clerical investiture.

All in all, Henry was a wise ruler and a skilled diplomatist. His brother Robert returned from the Crusade but proved to be such an inefficient ruler of his duchy that his subjects revolted and asked for Henry's aid. Robert was taken prisoner and spent the rest of his long life in Cardiff Castle.

Queen Matilda died at Westminster on 1 May 1118. Two years later, on 25 November 1120, Henry's only legitimate son, William, was drowned with a large entourage in the wreck of the White Ship crossing the channel from Normandy. The news so grieved the king that it was said he never smiled again. In the hope of having further legitimate issue, Henry remarried in 1122. His bride was Adeliza, daughter of Godfrey, Count of Louvain, but the marriage was childless and at Christmas 1126 Henry designated his daughter Matilda, widow of the Emperor Henry V, to be his heir and chose a second husband for her in the person of Geoffrey Plantagenet, son of Fulk V, Count of Anjou. Although William and Matilda were Henry's only legitimate offspring, he left a large illegitimate progeny of 21 or more children, among them Robert, Earl of Gloucester, who was to champion his half-sister Matilda in her claim to the throne.

21. Henry I, from a series of seventeenth-century portraits by an unknown artist.

Henry left England for Normandy in August 1135 and at the end of November was staying at his royal hunting-box at St Denis-le-Fermont, near Gisors, where he supped injudiciously on lampreys, 'which always disagreed with him, although he was excessively fond of them'. Ptomaine poisoning ensued and the king died on 1 December 1135, aged 67. His body was returned to England and buried in his foundation, Reading Abbey. No trace of his tomb has survived and the probable site is covered by a car park.

STEPHEN
1135–54

Although Stephen had been among the barons to swear to acknowledge his cousin Matilda as heiress to England and Normandy, he left Boulogne immediately on hearing of his uncle's death and went to London, where he gathered support and, claiming that Henry had changed his mind on his deathbed, induced the Archbishop of Canterbury (William de Corbeil) to crown him king at Westminster Abbey on St Stephen's Day, 26 December 1135. The concept of a female sovereign was so strange that it took little to convince people that Stephen's claim was just.

Stephen was the third son of Stephen, Count of Blois and Chartres, and his wife Adela, one of William the Conqueror's daughters, and was born at Blois in about 1096. As a young man he spent much time at the court of his uncle King Henry I, with whom he became a great favourite, and in 1125 he married Matilda, only daughter and heiress of Eustace III, Count of Boulogne, and Mary of Scotland, the sister of Henry I's first queen.

The Empress Matilda at once protested against Stephen's usurpation, but he was recognised by Pope Innocent II and with the aid of his brother Henry, Bishop of Winchester, secured the royal treasury and set

22. Stephen, from a series of seventeenth-century portraits. Coins of his reign depict Stephen as a bearded figure.

about bribing many of his opponents. Various baronial insurrections and wars with the Scots occupied the first few years of Stephen's troubled reign, but he won a victory over the Scots at the Battle of the Standard in August 1138 and a peace was concluded.

Meanwhile, Matilda had been gathering her forces and landed in England in the autumn of 1139. She was joined by her half-brother Robert, Earl of Gloucester, and other powerful barons and in the course of the ensuing wars Stephen was captured at Lincoln in February 1141 and imprisoned at Bristol. His brother Henry turned against him and Matilda was proclaimed 'Lady of the English' by a legatine council of the English Church held at Winchester on 7 April 1141; but, although she was in possession of the royal regalia, she was never crowned.

Stephen's supporters captured Robert of Gloucester and exchanged him for Stephen. The fighting continued for several years with no decisive outcome. On one occasion Matilda escaped from Devizes disguised as a corpse and on another from Oxford Castle by lowering herself on a rope and wearing a white cloak to blend into the snow-covered landscape. In 1144 her husband Geoffrey Plantagenet conquered Normandy and a few years later Matilda joined him there.

In 1153 Matilda's eldest son Henry took her place and rallied her old supporters, but the matter was settled without bloodshed and it was agreed by the Treaty of Westminster that Stephen should retain the crown for life and that Henry should succeed him.

Stephen was a weak character, although not lacking in courage, and his wife Matilda was his superior in every way. Her death at Hedingham Castle, Essex, on 3 May 1152 left Stephen without any spirit to continue the dynastic struggle and he was only too willing to conclude the Treaty of Westminster. He died at Dover Castle on 25 October 1154, apparently from appendicitis, and was buried with his wife and their son Eustace at Faversham Abbey, which he had founded. His two surviving children, William and Mary, successively held their mother's county of Boulogne.

THE ANGEVINS

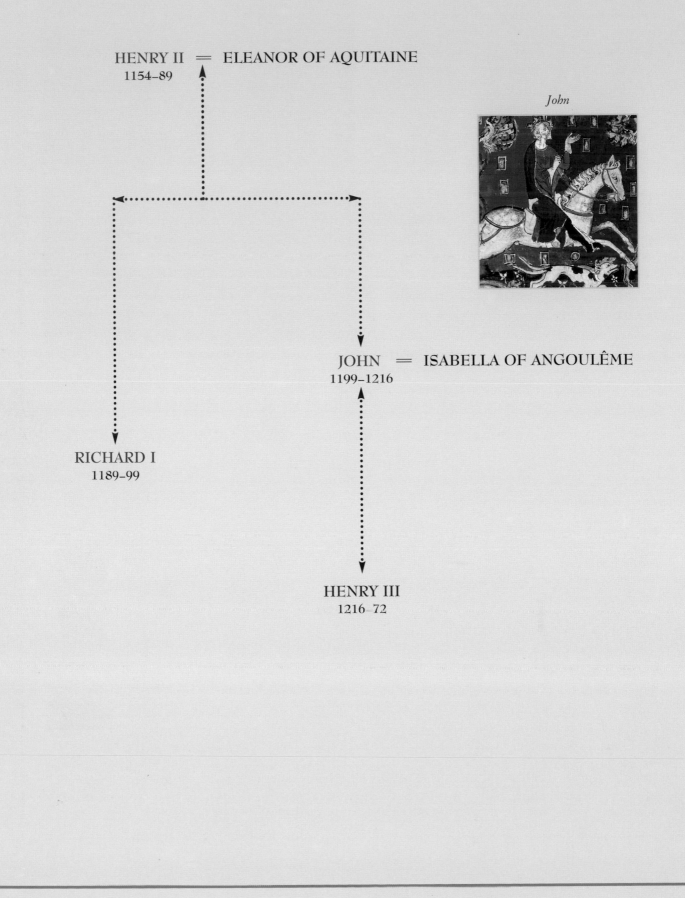

HENRY II $=$ ELEANOR OF AQUITAINE
1154–89

John

JOHN $=$ ISABELLA OF ANGOULÊME
1199–1216

RICHARD I
1189–99

HENRY III
1216–72

HENRY II
1154–89

The eldest of the three sons of the Empress Matilda and her second husband Geoffrey Plantagenet, Count of Anjou and Maine, was born at Le Mans on 25 March 1133 and named after his maternal grandfather King Henry I. In his youth he was known as Henry Fitz-Empress, but later he was to acquire the nickname of 'Curtmantle' from the short cloak he wore at a time when much longer ones were in vogue in England.

Henry's father captured Normandy while Stephen was preoccupied with the war with Matilda in England, and in 1150 Henry was invested with the duchy. Geoffrey died in the following year and Henry succeeded to the counties of Anjou and Maine, laying the foundation for a vast continental empire, to which the duchy of Aquitaine was to be added following Henry's marriage at Bordeaux on 18 May 1152 to its Duchess Eleanor, whose previous marriage to King Louis VII of France had been annulled on the grounds of consanguinity. She was Henry's senior by about 11 years and had gained a reputation for frivolity and looseness of conduct when she accompanied her first husband to the Holy Land on crusade. Her relationship with Henry was tempestuous, although five sons and three daughters were born in the first 15 years of their marriage.

The civil war in England was ended by the Treaty of Westminster in 1153, and on Stephen's death in October 1154 Henry's accession was accepted unopposed. He was crowned at Westminster Abbey on 19 December 1154. Eleanor was in an advanced stage of pregnancy at the time and her coronation did not take place until 25 December 1158, when she was crowned at Worcester Cathedral, declaring afterwards, with reference to her first marriage, 'I am Queen of England by the wrath of God.'

Henry spent the first years of his reign restoring law and order to the country, which had suffered much under Stephen's lax rule. He was ably assisted by his Chancellor, Thomas à Becket, who was appointed Archbishop of Canterbury in 1162, at a time when Henry was absent in France about the affairs of his continental possessions. After the king's return to England in 1163, he and Becket fell out over the question of whether clergy who committed crimes should be tried in civil or Church courts. Becket refused to comply with Henry's wishes in this matter and was accordingly deprived of his revenues and exiled to France in 1164. A reconciliation was forced by the threat of a papal interdict in 1170 and Becket returned to be reinstated, though not for long. Henry's exasperated utterance, 'Will no one rid me of this turbulent priest?' led to Becket's murder in his own cathedral by four of Henry's knights on 29 December 1170. The king was stricken with remorse over this deed and did public penance at Becket's tomb, which was soon to become a shrine and a place of pilgrimage.

23. Cast of Henry II's monumental effigy in the abbey church of Fontévrault.

Earlier in 1170 Henry had caused his second but eldest surviving son and heir, also named Henry and then aged 15, to be crowned at West-minster Abbey on 14 June, emulating a French practice for ensuring the succession. The boy had been married since the age of five to Margaret, a daughter of his mother's first husband Louis VII by a subsequent wife. The French king took exception to the fact that his daughter had not been crowned with her husband and to appease him the ceremony was repeated at Winchester Cathedral on 27 August 1172. 'The Young King', as he was called, was allowed no part in government. He rebelled against his father, but they were eventually reconciled. In 1182 he fought against his brother Richard, but on 11 June 1183 he died of fever in France. He left no surviving issue and his widow married King Béla III of Hungary.

The closing years of Henry's reign were taken up by quarrels with his surviving sons, who were incited to rebel against him by their mother Queen Eleanor, from whom Henry had separated. In 1189 he received the news at Tours that his youngest and favourite son John was siding with his enemies. Heartbroken and prematurely aged at 56, he set out to meet King Philip II of France. While they were speaking, still seated on their horses, a clap of thunder caused Henry's horse to rear and throw him. Badly shaken, he was carried on a litter to the castle of Chinon, where he died on 6 July 1189, calling for heaven's vengeance on his rebellious family. He was buried in the abbey church at Fontévrault, where his restored effigy may still be seen and, though stylised, gives a good impression of his general appearance. Queen Eleanor lived on for many years and died at Fontévrault on 31 March or 1 April 1204, aged about 82. She was buried beside Henry.

RICHARD I
1189–99

Richard Lionheart (or Coeur de Lion, to express his nickname in the original French) was the third son and fourth child of Henry II and Eleanor. He was born at Beaumont Palace, Oxford, on 8 September 1157. In 1172, before reaching the age of 15, he was invested with his mother's duchy of Aquitaine and in 1179 showed his military prowess by taking the allegedly impregnable fortress of Taillebourg from the French. Four years later he became heir apparent to his father's dominions on the death of Henry 'The Young King'.

In 1187 Richard set out to join the Third Crusade on hearing the news that Saladin had won an overwhelming victory over the Christian forces. Before leaving he had a stormy meeting with his father and King Philip II of France, to whom he did homage for his French possessions, to his father's great annoyance.

On learning of his father's death, Richard at once returned to England, stopping at Rouen en route to be invested with the duchy of Normandy and receive the homage of his Norman barons. He was crowned at Westminster Abbey on 3 September 1189, but the coronation festivities were marred by a massacre of London Jews, who had been forbidden to attend the coronation, followed by similar massacres in Lincoln, Norwich and York. Richard was only interested in raising money to pursue the Crusade, and returned to Normandy before Christmas. In July 1190 he and the French King Philip set out at the head of their troops to march across Europe.

By October they had reached Messina, where Richard did penance for an unspecified vice. Homosexuality has been suggested and seems likely, although disputed by a recent biographer. Richard's mother saw the necessity to provide him with a wife and selected Berengaria, daughter of Sancho VI, King of Navarre. Urged to comply, Richard agreed and his mother set out to escort Berengaria to join him. When they got to Messina, Eleanor handed Berengaria over to her daughter Joan, the widowed queen of Sicily, and the two younger women went on to join Richard, who had now reached Cyprus. Richard and Berengaria were married in the chapel of St George in Limasol Castle on 12 May 1191 and Berengaria was crowned as queen immediately following the ceremony. The marriage probably remained unconsummated.

The Crusade reached the Holy Land, but failed to recapture Jerusalem, although Acre was taken. In October 1192, after concluding a truce with Saladin, the Saracen leader, Richard and his party set out for home. His wife and sister travelled on a separate ship and landed safely at Naples, but Richard's ship was wrecked in the Adriatic and he decided to continue his journey by land. While in the Holy Land he had rashly insulted Duke Leopold of Austria and while crossing that monarch's dominions was recognised and thrown into prison, where he remained for 15 months

24. Richard I, after a bronze by Carlo Marochetti, exhibited at the Great Exhibition in 1851 and erected in Old Palace Yard, Westminster, in 1860.

until the ransom demanded was paid. A romantic legend tells of the minstrel Blondel seeking out Richard's place of imprisonment by wandering through Austria singing one of the king's own songs until the refrain was taken up from a barred window, and then gaining employment in the castle in order to negotiate the ransom.

Richard returned to England in March 1194 to find that his brother John had been depleting the treasury and was plotting to usurp the throne. John exerted his undoubted charm and his brother forgave him, exclaiming, 'You are a child.'

Richard only remained in England for a short time and then left for the Continent, where his territories were under threat. He constructed (to his own design it is said) the great fortress of Château-Gaillard to guard the border between Normandy and France.

In March 1199 Richard besieged the town of Châlus in Limousin, which the local landlord had refused to give up to him, although he claimed it as ultimate suzerain. While riding before the town walls one morning Richard was struck on the right shoulder by an arrow loosed from the battlements by a crossbowman. He made light of the wound and brought the siege to a successful conclusion a day or two later. His physician Marchadeus had made a bungling job of removing the arrow, however, and gangrene set in. Richard died on 6 April 1199, tenderly nursed by his mother, Queen Eleanor. He was buried beside his father at Fontévrault, his heart being buried separately at Rouen.

Richard spent less time in England than any other king, yet he has come to be regarded as a national hero and the archetype of English monarchy, commemorated by the fine equestrian statue erected outside the Houses of Parliament. Queen Berengaria, who never set foot in England, founded the Abbey of L'Epau, near Le Mans, and died there soon after 1230.

JOHN
1199–1216

John, the youngest son of Henry II and Queen Eleanor, was born at Beaumont Palace, Oxford, on 24 December 1167. He was the favourite child of both his parents, who indulged his every whim. Nevertheless, he received no patrimony and for that reason was nicknamed 'John Lackland'. He grew up a dandy, a gourmet, a womaniser, and entirely unprincipled.

When Richard I became king in 1189 he conferred the county of Mortain in Normandy upon John and also arranged his marriage on 29 August 1189 to a great heiress, Isabella of Gloucester, granddaughter of Henry I's bastard son Robert, Earl of Gloucester, who had been such a staunch supporter of the Empress Matilda in her struggle with Stephen. As the couple were second cousins, the Archbishop of Canterbury declared the marriage void, but John appealed to the Pope and got the decision reversed. However, John and Isabella were quite incompatible and soon separated.

John was excluded from any part in the government when Richard departed on the Crusade, but he soon managed to win over the people of London and to expel William de Longchamp, the Chancellor, who had been appointed as principal regent. Richard always forgave John for his scheming against him and on his deathbed named him as heir, although by the law of primogeniture, Arthur, Duke of Brittany, the son of Geoffrey, John's elder brother, should have succeeded.

John was invested as Duke of Normandy at Rouen on 23 April 1199 and then set out for England, where he was crowned at Westminster Abbey on 27 May. He next obtained the annulment of his marriage to Isabella of Gloucester, who was never acknowledged as queen, and on 24 August 1200 married at Bordeaux another Isabella, the 12-year-old daughter and heiress of Aymer Taillefer, Count of Angoulême. They returned to England and Isabella was duly crowned queen at Westminster on 8 October 1200. In spite of an age disparity of over 20 years, she proved a suitable consort for John, both being frivolous and pleasure-loving. Neither was particularly faithful to the other and on one occasion John is said to have hanged one of Isabella's supposed lovers over her bed. After the queen had borne three children John's suspicions of her infidelity caused him to place her in confinement in 1212, but a year later they were reconciled and two more children were subsequently born.

John must be held responsible for the murder of his nephew and potential rival Arthur in 1203, a deed that aroused the fury of King Philip of France, overlord of both Normandy and Brittany. He declared John's duchy of Normandy to be forfeited and led an invasion, taking Rouen in June 1204.

At home John began a quarrel with the Holy See on the old question of nomination to bishoprics. It led to his excommunication and a general interdict, which lasted from 1208 until 1213, when John gave in and was obliged to humiliate himself at the feet of Stephen Langton, Archbishop of Canterbury, the nominee of Pope Innocent III.

Another disastrous campaign in France was waged in 1214 and during John's absence from England his barons united together under Langton to protest against the longstanding misgovernment of the realm. The result was the best known event of John's reign, his forced sealing of Magna Carta at Runnymede, near Windsor, on 15 June 1215. The Great Charter defined the rights of the Church, the barons and the people. John claimed that he had sealed the charter under duress, which was true, and gained permission from his erstwhile enemy the Pope to raise an army to fight the barons. The barons invited Louis, the son and heir of the French king, to come over and lead them and a year of indecisive civil war followed.

While journeying through East Anglia with his army, John attempted to cross the Wash from Norfolk to Lincolnshire, but misjudged the tides so that the whole of his baggage train was swept away, including his crown and many valuables. This so upset John that he became ill with fever, which he aggravated by a gluttonous consumption of peaches and new cider. The next day he was suffering from dysentery, but he managed to ride to Sleaford and thence proceeded by litter to Newark Castle, where he died a few days later on 18 October 1216, aged nearly 49. He was robed as a monk and buried in Worcester Cathedral, where his tomb may still be seen surmounted by a non-contemporary effigy.

John has gone down in history as the archetypal bad king, cruel and avaricious, but he did have some redeeming qualities, possessing a sense of humour and being capable of occasional acts of mercy and generosity.

Queen Isabella, after assuring the succession of her son Henry and the safety of her children, returned to France in 1217 to reside in her county of Angoulême. In 1220 she married Hugh de Lusignan, Count of La Marche, to whom she had been betrothed as a child before her marriage to John, and bore a large second family. Several of her sons came to England and figured prominently at the court of their half-brother Henry III. In 1242 Isabella left Hugh de Lusignan and entered the abbey of Fontévrault, where she died on 31 May 1246. She was buried in the abbey graveyard, but when Henry III visited the abbey some years later he caused her body to be reburied in the choir of the abbey church and commissioned the effigy which is still to be seen beside those of Henry II, Eleanor of Aquitaine and Richard I.

25. *An illumination from the 13th-century manuscript* De Rege Johanne, *showing King John riding in a stag hunt.*

THE PLANTAGENETS

HENRY III = ELEANOR OF PROVENCE
1216–72

EDWARD I = ELEANOR OF CASTILE
1272–1307

EDWARD II = ISABELLA OF FRANCE
1307–27

EDWARD III = PHILIPPA OF HAINAULT
1327–77

EDWARD = JOAN OF KENT
'THE BLACK
PRINCE'
D.1376

RICHARD II
1377–99

EDMUND OF LANGLEY
DUKE OF YORK

RICHARD OF CONISBURGH
EARL OF CAMBRIDGE

RICHARD
DUKE OF YORK

EDWARD IV
1461–70
1471–83

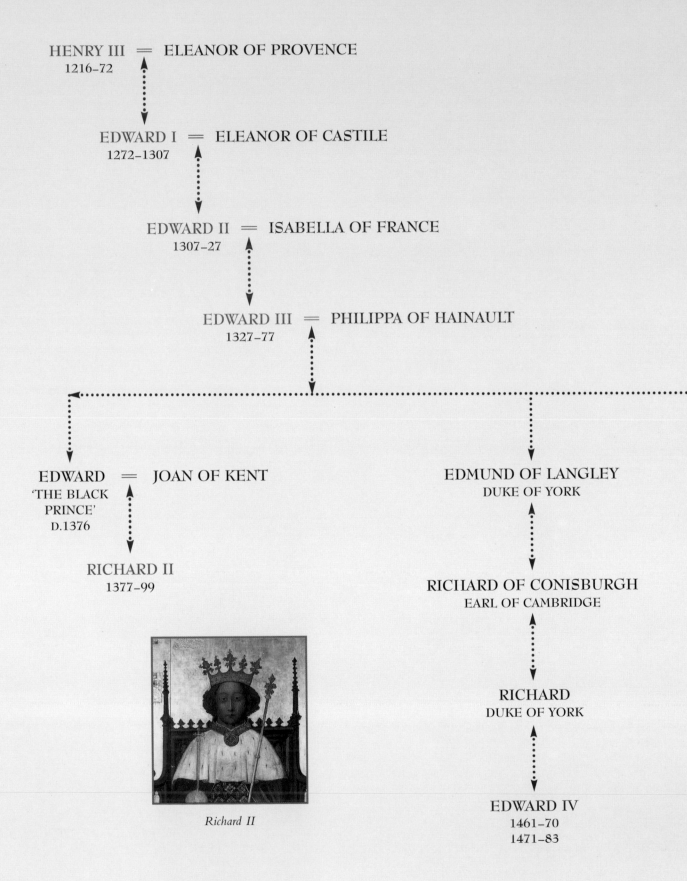

Richard II

HENRY III
1216–72

Henry, the elder son of John and Isabella of Angoulême, was born at Winchester Castle on 1 October 1207. He was living at Gloucester with his mother, brother and three sisters when his father's death brought him to the throne at the age of nine. The greater part of eastern England was in the hands of the rebel barons, so Henry was crowned in Gloucester Cathedral on 28 October 1216. Since the regalia remained at Westminster and John's personal crown had been lost in the Wash, the young king's crown was a golden torque (or bracelet, according to some accounts) belonging to his mother. The regency was undertaken by William Marshal, Earl of Pembroke, until his death in 1219 and then by Hubert de Burgh. By the end of 1217 the French invaders were forced to withdraw and the barons brought to heel. On 17 May 1220 Henry was crowned again with full ceremonial in Westminster Abbey. He was formally declared of age in 1223, but his personal rule did not commence until 1227.

Henry was a weak, indecisive character, easily led by others. His extortionate taxation, disastrous foreign policy, and the appointment of his half-brothers and his wife's relations to high positions led to unrest and further civil war with the barons, led by Henry's brother-in-law Simon de Montfort, Earl of Leicester. The king and his son Edward were defeated and captured at Lewes in 1264 and Henry was forced to summon a Parliament. While the king submitted, his son carried on the fight and at the battle of Evesham in 1265 Simon de Montfort was killed. Peace was concluded with the remaining rebels and the king became a mere cipher, all power passing to his son and his brother Richard of Cornwall, both much stronger characters.

What Henry lacked in statesmanship was compensated for by his piety and his patronage of literature and the arts. To him we owe the rebuilding of Westminster Abbey as a tribute to his profound veneration of Edward the Confessor, whose remains he personally assisted in carrying to their new shrine on 13 October 1269.

Henry was married at Canterbury Cathedral on 4 January 1236 to Eleanor, the second daughter and co-heiress of Raymond Berenger V, Count of Provence. She was crowned at Westminster Abbey on 20 January and, although a

BLANCHE OF LANCASTER = **JOHN OF GAUNT**

HENRY IV
1399–1413

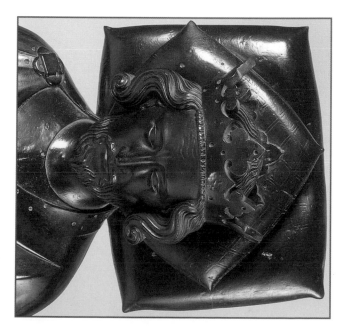

26. An electrotype of Henry III's monumental effigy of c.1291 in Westminster Abbey, where he was buried close to the shrine of Edward the Confessor, encased in that king's original coffin.

woman of great beauty and a faithful and devoted wife to the equally faithful Henry, rendered herself unpopular by her extravagance and her pro-
curement of great offices for her maternal uncles, Peter and Boniface of
Savoy, the latter of whom became Archbishop of Canterbury. The marriage
produced six sons (of whom only two survived infancy) and three daughters (of whom again two survived).

Henry was greatly stricken by the death of his beloved brother
Richard in April 1272 and soon thereafter exhibited signs of senility. He
died at the Palace of Westminster on 16 November 1272, aged 65, after a
reign of 56 years, one of the longest in English history. He was buried in
Westminster Abbey near the Confessor's shrine and his heart was sent to
Fontévrault. Henry's fine tomb effigy probably presents a genuine, if somewhat stylised, likeness.

Queen Eleanor exercised the regency until her son Edward returned
from the Crusades in 1274. Six years later she retired to the Benedictine
convent at Amesbury, where she took the veil after obtaining the Pope's
permission to retain her dower. She died there on 24 June 1291, aged
about 68, and was buried in the convent church minus her heart, which
was buried in the church of the Friars Minor (Minories) in London.

EDWARD I
1272–1307

Edward, the eldest child of Henry III and Eleanor of Provence, was
born at the Palace of Westminster on 17 June 1239. He was destined
to become the outstanding English warrior king of the Middle Ages and
fortunately inherited none of his father's weaknesses, taking instead after
his able uncle Richard of Cornwall. He also possessed his mother's strength
of character, untempered by her frivolity.

At the age of 15, Edward travelled to Spain with his mother and was
married at Las Huelgas in October 1254 to the Infanta Leonor (known as
Eleanor in England), daughter of Fernando III, King of Castile and León.
It was to prove an even greater love match than that of Edward's parents
and the couple were inseparable for the rest of their joint lives.

*27. A contemporary drawing of Edward I,
from a memoranda roll.*

After supporting his father throughout the civil wars, Edward set out
to join the Crusades in 1270 and the romantic (though probably untrue) story is told of Eleanor sucking the poison
from his wounded arm after he had been struck with a poisoned dagger. When Henry III died in 1272 the couple had
reached Sicily on their return journey, which they completed in leisurely fashion. They were crowned together at
Westminster Abbey on 19 August 1274, the first king and queen to be crowned together since the Conquest.

Edward's warlike character did not allow him to rest for long and he was soon campaigning to assert his overlordship of Scotland, which he continued to do for many years. It won him the soubriquet the 'Hammer of the Scots',
which was inscribed on his tomb. He also completely subjugated Wales in two wars and initiated a policy of castle
building to maintain English rule there. In a less warlike vein Edward summoned parliaments, laying the foundation
for the form of parliamentary government that has existed ever since.

The news of the death of Queen Margaret of Scotland ('The Maid of Norway') in 1290 sent Edward hurrying
north to attempt to settle the question of the succession there. Queen Eleanor followed him in more leisurely fashion,
but fell ill with fever on the way and was lodged at Harby, near Lincoln. Her constitution had been undermined by
frequent childbearing (at least 16 pregnancies can be accounted for in the course of her marriage) and she died on 24

28. An electrotype of the monumental effigy of c.1291–3 of Edward I's first queen, Eleanor of Castile, in Westminster Abbey.

November 1290, aged about 49. The grief-stricken king, who had been recalled, arrived too late. He escorted her body back to London in slow stages, erecting memorial crosses, 12 in number, at the places where her body rested overnight. A replica of the last of these may be seen in the forecourt of Charing Cross Station. Eleanor was buried at the feet of her father-in-law Henry III. Her effigy still conveys something of the serenity and beauty that captivated the king.

Edward remained a widower for nine years and then married, at the age of 60, Margaret, daughter of Philip III, King of France. The bride landed at Dover on 8 September 1299 and the marriage took place at Canterbury Cathedral two days later. In spite of an age difference of some 40 years the marriage was not unhappy and three children were born.

In 1307 Edward was again campaigning in the north when he was struck down by dysentery and died at Burgh-on-the-Sands, near Carlisle, on 7 July, having just completed his 68th year, a remarkable age for that era. He was taken back to Westminster to be buried near his father and his first wife. In stark contrast to theirs, his tomb is without an effigy and completely unadorned.

Queen Margaret died at Marlborough Castle, where she had resided during her widowhood, on 14 February 1317. She was buried in the church of the Grey Friars in London, of which she was a co-founder. Her monument, and those of nine other members of the royal family interred there, was sold for £50 by an avaricious Lord Mayor in the reign of Elizabeth I and subsequently lost.

EDWARD II
1307–27

Edward of Caernarvon, as he was known from his birthplace, was the youngest child of Edward I and Eleanor of Castile. He was born at Caernarvon Castle on 25 April 1284 and the well-known (though apocryphal) legend has it that his father presented the baby on his shield to the people of Wales as a prince who could speak no English.

Edward did not become heir apparent until the death of his elder brother, Alfonso, Earl of Chester, when he was four months old, and was not created Prince of Wales and Earl of Chester until 7 February 1301.

Since Edward lost his mother at the age of six and did not acquire a stepmother for another nine years, he lacked parental guidance for most of his childhood and his longing for companions of his own age and sex was probably engendered at this early stage of his life. His first 'favourite' was Piers Gaveston, a Gascon, who became his inseparable

29. Edward II's effigy on his tomb in Gloucester Cathedral, dated c.1330.

companion and alienated most of the court by applying sarcastic and offensive nicknames to its members. On Edward's accession in 1307 he conferred the royal earldom of Cornwall on his favourite.

Before his father's death Edward had been betrothed to Isabelle, the eldest daughter of Philip IV, King of France, and Jeanne I, Queen of Navarre, and in January 1308, accompanied by his stepmother, Queen Margaret (the bride's aunt), he set out for Boulogne to complete the marriage, leaving Gaveston as regent in England. The marriage was celebrated with great pomp on 25 January and after several days of feasting the couple set out to return to England. They were met at Dover by Gaveston and the very open display of affection between him and the king caused great dismay to Isabelle and her two uncles, who had accompanied them.

The coronation took place at Westminster Abbey on 25 February. Gaveston carried the crown and, it was said, 'was dressed more magnificently than the sovereign himself.' Feeling against the favourite ran high until finally he was kidnapped by the Earl of Warwick and beheaded in 1312. The king hid his feelings by the callous comment: 'By God, what a fool he was! I could have told him never to get into Warwick's hands.'

In 1314 Edward decided to renew his father's Scottish campaign, but was soundly defeated at Bannockburn by the forces of Robert Bruce, who thus finally secured Scottish independence.

The king acquired a new favourite in the person of Hugh le Despenser, who with his father, Hugh 'the elder', Earl of Winchester, supported Edward against the coalition of nobles, the 'Lords Ordainers', formed in 1310. They also intrigued against Queen Isabelle and induced the king to deprive her of her estates in 1324. Furious at this, she went to France the following year and joined her lover, Roger Mortimer. They raised an army and returned in 1326, carrying all before them. Edward was deposed on 20 January 1327 and confined in Berkeley Castle, where some nine months later he was barbarously murdered by the insertion of a red hot iron 'into his entrailes'. His unmarked body was taken to Gloucester Cathedral for burial and a beautiful alabaster effigy was placed over his tomb by his son, Edward III. It has been badly vandalised over the years by people carving their initials.

The murder brought about a surge of public feeling against Queen Isabelle, the 'she-wolf of France' as she became known. Mortimer was snatched from her side by her son King Edward in spite of her cry, 'Fair son, have mercy on the gentle Mortimer!' He was to have the distinction of being the first person to be executed at Tyburn. Isabelle was obliged to live in retirement at Castle Rising in Norfolk, where she died on 22 August 1358. She was buried not far from Mortimer in Grey Friars Church, London, 'with the heart of her murdered husband on her breast.'

EDWARD III
1327–77

Edward was the eldest of the four children of Edward II and Isabelle of France. He was born at Windsor Castle on 13 November 1312 at 5.40 a.m. and was the first English king to have the exact time of his birth noted. A few days later he was created Earl of Chester by his father, but not, for some reason, Prince of Wales.

Edward was proclaimed Keeper of the Realm on 26 October 1326 and king on 25 January 1327, following his father's deposition five days earlier. His coronation at Westminster Abbey took place on 2 February.

On 24 January 1328 Edward was married at York Minster to Philippa, the third daughter of William III, Count of Holland and Hainault. She was his senior by about a year and five months and had first been considered as a possible bride when she was eight and he seven. They had met when Edward and his mother were guests at the court of Hainault in 1326 and a papal dispensation for the marriage was obtained from Avignon in September 1327. The new queen was crowned at Westminster Abbey on 20 February 1328. It was an excellent match and in the course of 25 years was to produce 12 children. Philippa was plump and homely and endowed with a kindly nature that rendered her popular with her subjects and enabled her to exert a restraining influence on her husband and eldest son when their tempers got the better of them. She is perhaps best known for the episode in which she pleaded successfully for the lives of the six burghers of Calais who surrendered that town to Edward III.

Edward's long reign of 50 years was to be preoccupied by his claim to the throne of France, which began the Hundred Years War. He assumed the title of King of France in 1340, claiming the crown through his mother as heir of

30. Edward III, from a series of seventeenth-century likenesses of English kings by an unknown artist.

her brother Charles IV, who had died in 1328. The Salic Law which prevailed in France decreed that succession to the throne could not pass to or through a female and Charles had been succeeded by his cousin Philip VI, the nearest male heir. Edward had accepted this by doing homage for his French possessions in 1329 and 1331, but some years later, English commercial interests connected with the wool trade in Flanders precipitated a crisis. The Flemish weavers concluded a commercial treaty with Edward in 1338 and persuaded him to advance his claim to France.

The French king's answer to Edward's pretensions was to declare his French possessions forfeited and to invade Guienne. Edward defended his title by sea and land. The naval battle of Sluys in 1340 gave England control of the Channel, and was followed by the land victories of Crécy (1346) and Poitiers (1356). Calais was taken after a long siege in 1347.

The hero of the wars was Edward's eldest son, Edward of Woodstock, Prince of Wales, later to be known as 'the Black Prince', who was regarded as the 'model of chivalry' although in reality he was bad-tempered, foul-mouthed and cruel.

In 1349 England was ravaged by the Black Death, an outbreak of bubonic plague, which is said to have halved the population and greatly undermined the military strength. The wars were ended for a time by the Treaty of Bretigny in 1360, whereby Edward renounced his claim to the French crown, but the claim was renewed in 1369. Poitou was recaptured but the French regained control of the Channel at the battle of La Rochelle in 1372 and successfully blocked English transport. When the Black Prince died of dysentery in 1376, English fortunes were at their lowest ebb and only the five fortified towns of Bordeaux, Bayonne, Brest, Calais and Cherbourg and their coastal lands remained, although France was in a ruinous state.

At home, Edward's reign saw many changes, the division of Parliament into two houses, the creation of the office of Justice of the Peace, and the replacing of French by English in the law courts. In 1348 Edward founded the Order of the Garter, destined to become one of the most prestigious orders of chivalry in Europe.

Queen Philippa died of a 'dropsical malady' at Windsor Castle on 14 August 1369. Her monumental effigy, though somewhat damaged, gives a good impression of this amiable queen. After her death the king acquired a rapacious mistress, Alice Perrers, who was to render his declining years a thorough misery. Edward died following a stroke at Sheen Palace on 21 June 1377. He was buried beside Philippa in Westminster Abbey and his funeral effigy is believed to have been modelled from a death mask.

RICHARD II
1377–99

Richard was the youngest son of Edward, Prince of Wales ('the Black Prince'), and his wife Joan, Countess of Kent ('the Fair Maid of Kent'), who was herself a granddaughter of Edward I and his second wife, Margaret of France. He was born at Bordeaux on 6 January 1367 and in accordance with custom was therefore known as Richard of Bordeaux. The death of his elder brother Edward of Angoulême in 1372 left him as his father's sole heir.

31. An electrotype from Philippa of Hainault's tomb in Westminster Abbey, showing the plump, motherly figure she had become by the end of her life.

32. Edward, Prince of Wales ('The Black Prince'), from an electrotype of his monumental effigy in Canterbury Cathedral.

After his father's death, Richard was created Prince of Wales, Duke of Cornwall and Earl of Chester by his grandfather, Edward III, on 20 November 1376 and seven months later succeeded to the throne on his grandfather's death. Although only ten years old, he was crowned at Westminster Abbey on 16 July 1377. The long ceremony, preceded by fasting, exhausted the child and he had to be carried from the Abbey to Westminster Hall on the shoulders of his attendants. During his minority the government was carried on by a council of regency.

In 1381 the Peasants' Revolt led by Wat Tyler against the imposition of a poll tax was the occasion for a remarkable act of bravery by Richard, who at the age of just 14 rode out to meet the rebels at Smithfield and was personally able to pacify them.

His minority ended in the following year and he was married at St Stephen's Chapel in the Palace of Westminster on 20 January 1382 to Anne of Bohemia, the daughter of the Emperor Charles IV. She was his senior by about eight months and Richard fell deeply and passionately in love with her. Unfortunately the marriage remained childless and the queen's death, probably from plague, at Sheen Palace on 3 June 1394 almost drove Richard wild with grief. The heir presumptive while Richard remained childless was Roger Mortimer, Earl of March, the grandson of his uncle Lionel of Antwerp, Duke of Clarence, but although the king recognised his claim in 1387, it was contested by his three surviving uncles, the Dukes of Lancaster, York and Gloucester, who were continually vying for power.

On 1 November 1396 Richard contracted a second marriage at Calais with Isabelle of France, the second daughter of King Charles VI and Isabella (or Isabeau, as she is usually called) of Bavaria. The new queen was just coming up to her seventh birthday, so there could be no prospect of any issue of the marriage for nine or ten years. Richard treated his child bride with great kindness and affection and she in her turn appears to have been very fond of him.

What Richard most needed was a father-figure and this was eventually supplied by Robert de Vere, 9th Earl of Oxford, successively created Marquess of Dublin and Duke of Ireland. His relationship with the king was probably quite innocent, but it aroused the intense jealousy of Richard's uncles and others, who contrived to have de Vere charged with treason. He was forced to flee to the Continent, where he was killed in a boar hunt in 1392.

After concluding peace with France, cemented by his second marriage in 1396, Richard turned his attention to attempting to do away with parliamentary government and establish a royal autocracy. It proved his undoing and he was deposed in favour of his cousin Henry Bolingbroke on 29 September 1399. He was imprisoned first at Leeds Castle and then at Pontefract Castle, where he completely lost the will to live and literally starved himself to death on or about 14 February 1400. To refute false rumours that he had been murdered, his body was brought to London and taken to Westminster exposed on an open bier. He was buried beside his beloved Anne and near the tomb of his grandparents in Edward the Confessor's Chapel.

The little Queen Isabelle, still only ten years old, was kept in confinement by Henry IV and deprived of her jewels before being allowed to return to France in July 1401. In 1406 she made a second marriage to her cousin Charles, Duke of Orléans. The marriage was a happy but short one and Isabelle died at Blois on 14 September 1409, a few hours after the birth of her first child.

33. The famous portrait of Richard II, in Westminster Abbey. It was probably painted to commemorate the king's visit to the abbey on 13 October 1390 and is the first contemporary painted portrait of an English king.

34. An electrotype from the monumental effigy of Richard II's first queen, Anne of Bohemia, in Westminster Abbey.

THE
HOUSE OF LANCASTER

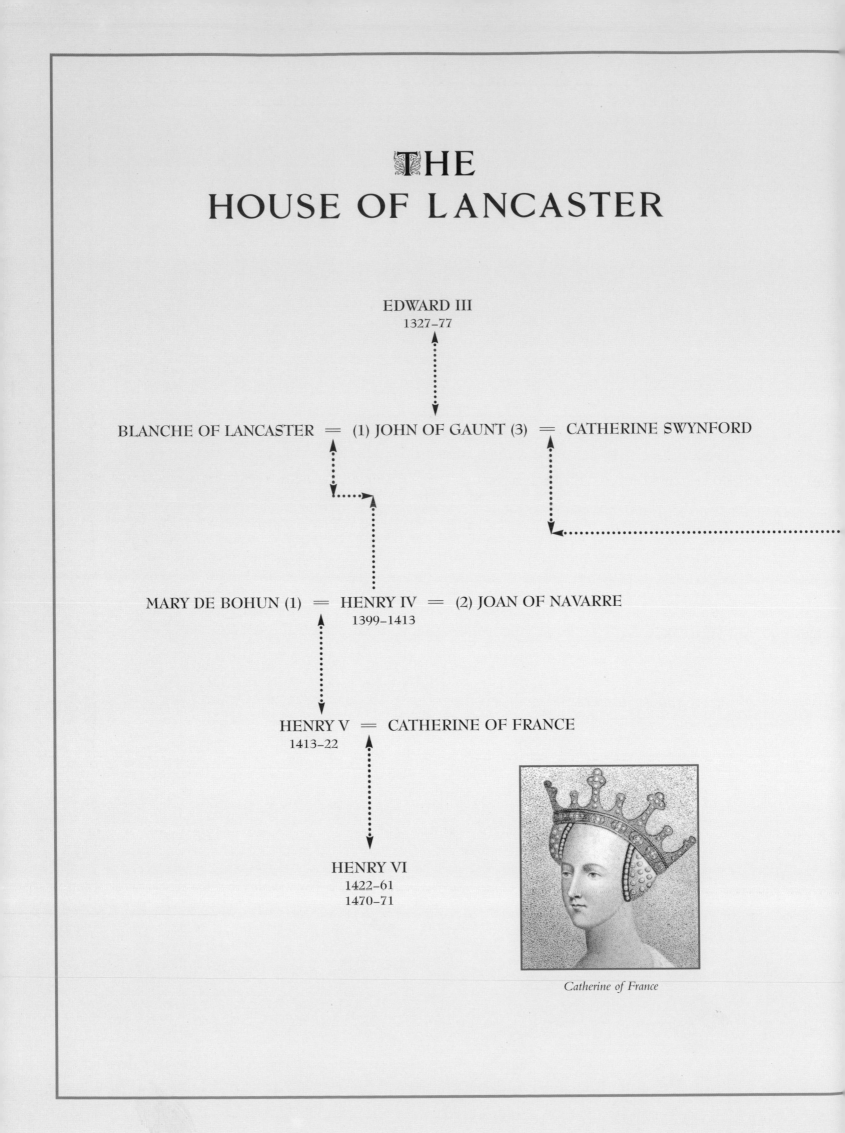

EDWARD III
1327–77

BLANCHE OF LANCASTER = (1) JOHN OF GAUNT (3) = CATHERINE SWYNFORD

MARY DE BOHUN (1) = HENRY IV = (2) JOAN OF NAVARRE
1399–1413

HENRY V = CATHERINE OF FRANCE
1413–22

HENRY VI
1422–61
1470–71

Catherine of France

HENRY IV
1399–1413

Henry was the fourth son of John of Gaunt, Duke of Lancaster (himself the fourth son of Edward III), and his first wife Blanche, younger daughter and co-heiress of Henry, 4th Earl and 1st Duke of Lancaster (a great-grandson of Henry III). He was born at Bolingbroke Castle, Lincolnshire, on 4 April 1366 and hence was known as Henry of Bolingbroke. Following the deaths of his three elder brothers, he became his father's heir and bore the courtesy title of Earl of Derby. At the age of 14 he was married at Arundel Castle in 1380 or 1381 to an 11-year-old heiress, Mary, daughter of Humphrey de Bohun, 7th Earl of Hereford, 6th Earl of Essex and 2nd Earl of Northampton. After bearing seven children she died following the birth of the last at Peterborough Castle on 4 July 1394.

35. An electrotype of the alabaster effigy of Henry IV in Canterbury Cathedral. The effigy agrees well with contemporary descriptions of the king.

JOHN BEAUFORT
EARL OF SOMERSET

JOHN BEAUFORT
DUKE OF SOMERSET

MARGARET BEAUFORT = EDMUND TUDOR
EARL OF RICHMOND

HENRY VII
1485–1509

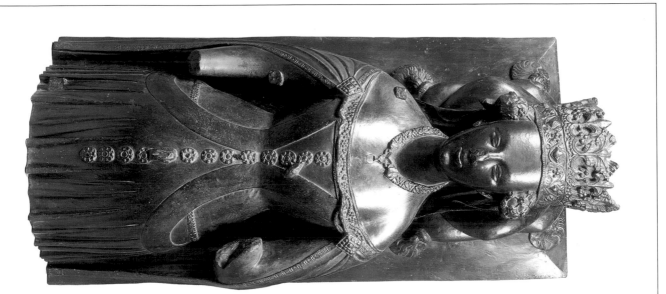

36. Henry IV's queen, Joan of Navarre, from an electrotype of her alabaster effigy in Canterbury Cathedral.
Henry and Joan were the only king and queen to be buried together at Canterbury.

After his wife's death Henry set off to see something of the world and visited Venice, Cyprus and Jerusalem, as well as serving for a spell with the Teutonic Knights in Lithuania. Having returned to England, he sided with his father and Richard II against Thomas of Woodstock, Duke of Gloucester, and was rewarded by being created Duke of Hereford in 1397. Early in 1398 he quarrelled with the Duke of Norfolk, who had accused him of treason, and the two dukes were about to settle the matter by combat when the king intervened and banished both of them from England.

Henry went to Paris, but on hearing of his father's death in February 1399 he returned secretly to recover his estates, which had been confiscated. He took advantage of the king's absence in Ireland to land in Yorkshire, where he was joined by the Percys. Richard was abandoned by his followers on his return and after surrendering at Flint was forced by Parliament to resign the crown to Henry on 29 September.

The new king was crowned at Westminster Abbey on 11 October 1399. The following year a bid for Welsh independence led by Owain Glyn Dwr began and took ten years to subdue. The French raided the south coast, the Scots made incursions in the north, and the Percys and the Mortimers led rebellions, supported by Archbishop Scrope of York, whose execution for treason was to label Henry as an impious monster. As if his troubled reign was not enough, Henry was also plagued with head lice and a disfiguring skin disease, referred to as 'leprosy' but probably a form of eczema.

Early in his reign Henry contracted a second marriage, by proxy at Eltham Palace on 3 April 1402 and in person at Winchester Cathedral on 7 February 1403, to Joan, widow of John V ('the Valiant'), Duke of Brittany, and daughter of Charles II ('the Bad'), King of Navarre. She was crowned queen at Westminster Abbey on 26 February. Although Joan was still in her early thirties and had borne nine children as Duchess of Brittany, there were no children by Henry and this fact, coupled with other dark rumours, led to accusations of witchcraft being made against the queen. It seems highly probable that she and her followers had brought some ancient Breton superstitions into England with them. Nevertheless, she formed an excellent relationship with her stepchildren, and Henry V was to term her 'his dearest mother' when he appointed her regent in 1417.

It had been prophesied that Henry IV would die in Jerusalem and he took comfort from the knowledge that his death would be deferred until he carried out his long-projected crusade. On 20 March 1413 he suffered a stroke while praying at Edward the Confessor's shrine in Westminster Abbey. He was carried to the Jerusalem Chamber near the west door and on regaining consciousness asked where he was. On being told he gave thanks to God, and saying, 'Now I know that I shall die here in this chamber,' very shortly expired.

Although he died at Westminster Abbey, Henry had expressed a wish to be buried at Canterbury Cathedral near the shrine of St Thomas à Becket. His body was conveyed there by land and water and his tomb, surmounted by his and Joan's crowned alabaster effigies, survives with only minor damage.

Queen Joan survived Henry for over twenty years. She acted as regent in 1417, but in the following year when her stepson John, Duke of Bedford, was acting as regent, she was accused of witchcraft, deprived of her property and dower, and kept in close confinement until July 1422, when she was released and her dower was restored. She died at her favourite residence, Havering atte Bower, Essex, on 9 July 1437, aged about 67, and was buried with Henry.

HENRY V
1413–22

Henry was the second, but first surviving, son of Henry IV and his first wife, Mary de Bohun. He was born at Monmouth on 16 December 1387 and hence was known as Henry of Monmouth. Two days after his father's coronation he was created Prince of Wales, Duke of Cornwall and Earl of Chester, and a month later Duke of Aquitaine and Duke of Lancaster.

The stories of his riotous youth are largely an invention of Shakespeare and not substantiated by any contemporary evidence. He had an early experience of armed combat during Owain Glyn Dwr's rebellion and at the age of 16 was wounded in the face by an arrow. His father's ill-health also obliged him to take some share in the government with his half-uncles the Beauforts (sons of John of Gaunt and his third wife, Catherine Swynford).

Henry succeeded his father and was crowned at Westminster Abbey on 9 April 1413. Shortly thereafter he decided to renew the French war begun by Edward III and the great battle of Agincourt, fought and won on 25 October 1415, was followed by a long campaign in the course of which many towns and villages were laid waste. Normandy was reconquered, and by August 1419 the gates of Paris had been reached. Negotiations for peace led to the Treaty of Troyes, whereby Henry was recognised as heir and regent of France to the exclusion of the Dauphin, and received in marriage the mad King Charles VI's youngest daughter, Catherine, whose elder sister Isabelle had been the second wife of Richard II. The wedding took place at Troyes on 2 June 1420.

37. A late eighteenth-century engraving of Catherine of France, based on a contemporary manuscript source.

38. Henry V, painted by an unknown artist in the late 16th or early 17th century.
Several versions of this image exist.

Henry was now the dominant power in western Europe, the last great warrior king of the Middle Ages, but he was stern and humourless and his personality does not attract. The later portrait reproduced here reveals a lean, ascetic face with an over-large nose beneath a monkish haircut. There is a general air of fanaticism about him.

Henry's next project was to lead a new crusade to recover Jerusalem, but before it could get under way he fell ill with dysentery, an ever-present scourge of military life at the time, and died at Bois de Vincennes, near Paris, on 31 August 1422, aged 35. His body was dismembered, boiled in a cauldron and brought back to be buried in Westminster Abbey in a chantry chapel east of Edward the Confessor's shrine. The effigy on his tomb was greatly damaged over the years, losing its head, but recently it has been carefully restored.

Queen Catherine returned to England with her husband's body and in 1424 took up residence at Baynard's Castle on the south bank of the Thames. Here she fell in love with Owen Tudor, a young Welsh squire of no fortune, and is alleged to have married him in secret, although no proof has ever been discovered. Three sons, Edmund, Jasper and Owen, were born over the next few years and in 1436 the queen gave birth to a daughter, Margaret, who did not survive. This last event brought Catherine's scandalous life to the knowledge of the king's guardians. Her sons were taken from her and she was forced to take up residence at Bermondsey Abbey, where she soon fell into a decline and died on 3 January 1437. She was buried at Westminster Abbey, but her mummified body was disinterred at the time of Henry VII's funeral and remained above ground in a chest for nearly three centuries. Samuel Pepys saw it when he visited the abbey in February 1669 and recorded in his diary that he 'did kiss her mouth, reflecting upon it that I did kiss a queen, and that this was my birthday, thirty-six years old, that I did first kiss a queen.' Catherine's body was eventually reburied in Henry V's Chantry.

HENRY VI
1422–61 and 1470–71

The only child of Henry V and Catherine of France was born at Windsor Castle on 6 December 1421 and named after his father and grandfather. He was only eight months old when his father's death made him king.

The baby king presided over Parliament seated in his mother's lap, but on one occasion in November 1423 he threw a great tantrum when being brought from Windsor and refused to be carried on from Staines, where he and his entourage had lodged overnight, delaying the slow progress to Westminster (with further overnight stops at Kingston and Kennington) by one day.

Henry was crowned at Westminster Abbey on 6 November 1429, exactly one month before his eighth birthday. Two years later, on 16 December 1431, he was also crowned king of France at Nôtre Dame Cathedral in Paris, being the only English claimant to the French throne to become de facto sovereign. Before he came of age, however, English rule in France began a steady decline with Joan of Arc's campaign and the death of the regent John, Duke of Bedford. By 1453 only Calais remained of Henry V's conquests.

The king was a pathetic figure, afflicted with periods of mental derangement in the same manner as his maternal grandfather, Charles VI of France. He was better fitted for a life of piety and learning than that of a monarch and is best remembered for his two great scholastic foundations, Eton College and King's College, Cambridge.

At the age of 23, in March 1445, Henry was married by proxy at Nancy and in person on 22 April at Titchfield Abbey, Hampshire, to Margaret of Anjou, daughter of René, Duke of Anjou and titular King of Naples and Sicily, and his first wife, Isabelle, in her own right Duchess of Lorraine. Queen Margaret was as strong and forceful as her husband was weak. The only child of the marriage, Edward, Prince of Wales, was born at the Palace of Westminster on 13 October 1453 during his father's first prolonged attack of insanity, in which Richard, 3rd Duke of York, the next in line to the throne after Henry and the infant prince, reigned as Protector. On the king's recovery in 1455, York was dismissed and Queen Margaret and Edmund Beaufort, Duke of Somerset, became all-powerful.

Open warfare between the rival branches of the royal family, the Lancastrians (whole emblem was the red rose) and the Yorkists (whose emblem was the white rose), soon broke out and Somerset was killed at the first battle of St Albans in May 1455. A peace of sorts was concluded, but four years later war recommenced and Henry was captured at Northampton in July 1460 and forced to recognise the Duke of York as his heir to the exclusion of his own son.

*39. A 16th-century copy of a contemporary portrait of Henry VI
in which his instability and weakness of character are apparent.*

Queen Margaret rallied the Lancastrian forces and won a victory at Wakefield in which Richard of York was slain on 29 December 1460, and the second battle of St Albans on 17 February 1461 secured Henry's release, although he was then in the throes of another bout of madness, laughing and singing insanely while the battle raged. The Lancastrian triumph was short-lived, however, for on 29 March 1461 the new Duke of York, Edward, defeated the royal forces in a snowstorm at Towton and Henry and Margaret fled to Scotland. Henry had already been formally deposed and York proclaimed king as Edward IV on 4 March.

Henry returned from Scotland in 1464 to take part in an abortive attempt to regain the throne, but was captured and imprisoned in the Tower of London, where he languished for six years until a brief restoration was engineered by Richard Neville, Earl of Warwick (known as 'Warwick the King-Maker'), on 3 October 1470. Henry's second reign, known as the 'readeption', lasted until 11 April 1471, when Edward, who had fled to Burgundy, where his sister was married to the reigning duke, returned and regained the throne.

Queen Margaret had joined forces with Warwick and betrothed her son Edward to his daughter Anne. They made their final stand against Edward at Tewkesbury and were defeated there on 4 May 1471. All the queen's hopes ended when her son was stabbed after the battle.

The hapless King Henry was returned to the Tower, where his death 'from pure displeasure and melancholy' (although it was widely believed he, too, had been stabbed) was announced on 21 May 1471. On the same day Queen Margaret was brought to the Tower and is said to have seen his body carried past her window. She was later removed to Wallingford Castle and released in November 1475 after her father had raised the ransom demanded by Edward IV. She returned to France and died in comparative poverty in the house of an old family retainer at Saumur on 25 August 1482, being buried with her parents in Angers Cathedral. Henry VI was buried first at Chertsey Abbey, but was later removed to St George's Chapel, Windsor, where his tomb consists of a plain black marble tablet bearing his name and the date in brass lettering. A cause for the canonisation of this most tragic of English kings has been made from time to time since his death.

THE HOUSE OF YORK

EDWARD III
1327–77

⇕

EDMUND OF LANGLEY
DUKE OF YORK

⇕

RICHARD OF CONISBURGII
EARL OF CAMBRIDGE

⇕

RICHARD
DUKE OF YORK
D. 1460

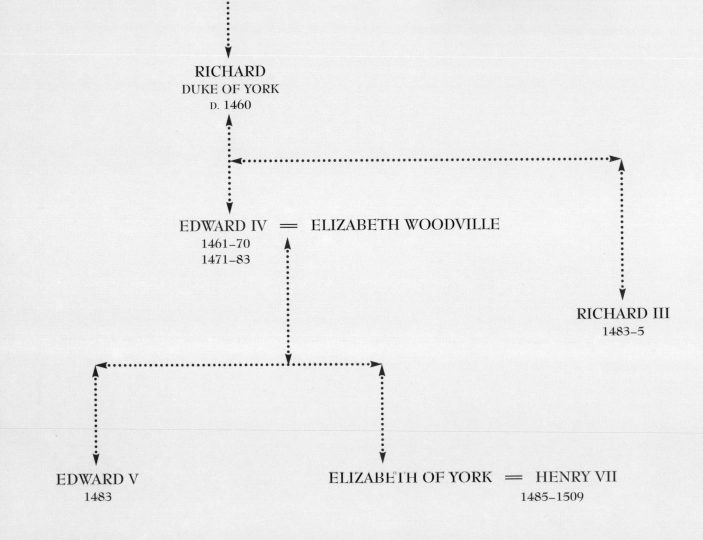

Richard III

EDWARD IV = ELIZABETH WOODVILLE
1461–70
1471–83

RICHARD III
1483–5

EDWARD V
1483

ELIZABETH OF YORK = HENRY VII
1485–1509

*40. Edward IV, by an unknown artist. His likeness
to his grandson Henry VIII is apparent in this portrait.*

EDWARD IV
1461–70 and 1471–83

Edward was the second son (an older brother Henry having died in infancy) of Richard, 3rd Duke of York, and his wife Cicely, twelfth and youngest daughter of Ralph Neville, 1st Earl of Westmorland, both parents descending from Edward III. He was born at Rouen, where his father was stationed on official duties, on 28 August 1442.

As soon as they were of an age to do so, Edward and his next brother, Edmund, took up arms in the Yorkist cause. Edmund was killed with their father at Wakefield in December 1460 and Edward succeeded as 4th Duke of York. On 4 March 1461 Henry VI was deposed and Edward was declared king in Parliament. He was crowned at Westminster Abbey on 29 June.

On 1 May 1464 Edward was married in a somewhat furtive manner at the parish church of Grafton Regis, Northamptonshire. His bride was Elizabeth, a lady some five years his senior and the widow of Sir John Grey, who was killed at the second battle of St Albans in 1461. Her father, Richard Woodville, later to be ennobled as Earl Rivers, was a country gentleman of undistinguished family, but her mother was Jacquette of Luxembourg, the widow of John, Duke of Bedford, the fourth son of Henry IV. Elizabeth had served as a maid of honour to Margaret of Anjou. The marriage to a lady of comparatively humble birth with such strong Lancastrian connections caused grave offence to Edward's brothers and other members of the court when it was presented to them as a fait accompli some months after it had taken place. Nevertheless, the new queen was crowned at Westminster Abbey with considerable pomp on 26 May 1465. The stately and aloof Elizabeth, who was already the mother of two sons by her first husband, presented the king with ten children, three sons and seven daughters.

In spite of his romantic marriage, Edward was a notorious womaniser and would pursue any woman who took his fancy, be she married or not. He abandoned his mistresses whenever he tired of them, but one who retained his favour was Jane (actually Elizabeth) Shore, the wife of a London merchant.

The king's marriage had caused Warwick 'the King-Maker' to switch his allegiance to the Lancastrians and re-open the civil war. After defeating Edward near Banbury in 1469, he went to France to raise more troops and returned to effect the 'readeption' of Henry VI (see p.73), forcing Edward to fly to France and the pregnant Queen Elizabeth and her children to seek Sanctuary at Westminster. The tables were turned in 1471 when Edward returned, and the slaying of Warwick at the battle of Barnet, followed soon after by the battle of Tewkesbury and the deaths of Henry VI and his son, put an end to Lancastrian hopes.

Edward's brother George, Duke of Clarence, had sided with his father-in-law, Warwick, and, although he changed sides again, was finally convicted of high treason and confined to the Tower of London, where he met his death in 1478, supposedly drowned in a butt of malmsey wine. How far Edward and his youngest brother, Richard, Duke of Gloucester, were implicated in his death is not known.

Edward was a popular and pleasure-loving monarch, eating and drinking to excess and then taking emetics so that he might start again. He had all the makings of a ruthless despot, however, and had he lived longer he might have become one of the most powerful of English kings. He was not quite 41 when he died at Westminster on 9 April 1483, probably of pneumonia caught on a fishing trip. He was buried at St George's Chapel, Windsor, under a simple black marble slab.

Queen Elizabeth's fate will be related in the story of her son's brief reign.

EDWARD V
April–June 1483

The eldest son of Edward IV and Elizabeth Woodville was born at Westminster on 4 November 1470, at a time when his father was in exile in Burgundy and his mother and her children had sought refuge in Sanctuary. In a few months all had changed and Edward IV was back on the throne and able to create his son Prince of Wales and Earl of Chester, Duke of Cornwall, Earl of March and Earl of Pembroke successively.

When his father died unexpectedly, the 12-year-old Prince Edward was residing at Ludlow, one of his official residences, and on receiving the news that he was now king set out for London, to be met on the way at Stony Stratford by his uncle Richard, Duke of Gloucester, on his way down from York. Richard conducted his nephew to London with every sign of loyalty and they were met outside the city by the Lord Mayor and leading citizens, who escorted them to the Tower, which it is alleged the young king never left again.

A sensation was caused some weeks later when Robert Stillington, Bishop of Bath and Wells and a former Chancellor openly hostile to the Woodvilles, questioned the validity of Edward IV's marriage to Elizabeth. Edward, it was claimed, had been pre-contracted to Lady Eleanor Butler, widow of Sir Thomas Butler and daughter of John Talbot, 1st Earl of Shrewsbury, and she was still living at the time of Edward's marriage to Elizabeth. The bishop's allegation may have been a complete fabrication, but it induced Parliament to declare Edward's marriage to Elizabeth invalid and their children bastards. It followed that Edward V was no longer king and he was declared deposed on 25 June 1483, his uncle Gloucester being proclaimed as Richard III in his place.

41. Edward V and his brother Richard, Duke of York. A sentimental Victorian concept of 'The Princes in the Tower' after Sir John Everett Millais.

One of the greatest unsolved historical mysteries now ensued – the fate of the 'Princes in the Tower'. Edward had been joined there by his younger and only surviving brother Richard, Duke of York, and the official version, engineered by Tudor propaganda, is that they were smothered in their sleep and buried beneath a staircase. The deed was carried out, at Richard III's behest, by Sir James Tyrrell, who later confessed under torture and was beheaded in 1502. No search for the bodies was made at the time and it was not until some repairs were being carried out in 1674 that the bones of two children were found beneath a staircase in the Tower. At Charles II's order they were placed in an urn and deposited in Westminster Abbey. Doubts as to the true fate of the princes were expressed from time to time, most notably by Horace Walpole in the eighteenth century. The bones were medically examined by Professor William Wright in 1933 and he came to the conclusion that they were those of two boys of corresponding age to those of the princes, but that it was impossible to establish beyond doubt that they were their remains.

42. *A sad-faced Richard III by an unknown artist, looking far from the monster his Tudor detractors would make him.*

There is some evidence that the princes were removed to Middleham Castle in Yorkshire and that they were still alive at the time of the Battle of Bosworth Field. If this were so, it follows that their deaths must have been ordered by Henry VII rather than by Richard. Controversy over the matter still rages. Josephine Tey's novel *The Daughter of Time* has done much to convince people of Richard III's innocence and this belief is furthered by the work of the Richard III Society.

A strange factor in the whole story is the attitude of the princes' mother Elizabeth, who appears to have been completely unconcerned as to their fate. She was reinstated as Queen Dowager in 1486, but her lands were forfeited in the following year for her alleged perfidy in attending Richard's court in 1484. She was obliged to retire to Bermondsey Abbey, where she died on 8 June 1492, aged about 55. She was buried with Edward IV in St George's Chapel, Windsor.

RICHARD III
1483–5

Richard was the eighth and youngest son of Richard Plantagenet, 3rd Duke of York, and his wife Cicely Neville. He was born at Fotheringay Castle, Northamptonshire, on 2 October 1452.

Richard was only eight years old when his brother Edward was proclaimed king and he was created Duke of Gloucester on the eve of Edward's coronation. He was a loyal and loving brother to the king and fought bravely in the later stages of the civil war, ending with the battle of Tewkesbury, following which his later denigrators were to allege he stabbed Henry VI's son Edward, Prince of Wales, with his own hand.

On 12 July 1472 Richard was married at Westminster to that Edward's widow, Anne, the younger daughter and co-heiress of Richard Neville, 1st Earl of Warwick ('the King-Maker'). Her elder sister Isabel had married Richard's brother George, Duke of Clarence, in 1469. These marriages caused a rift between the two brothers as George had hoped to retain all the Warwick estates for himself, and when he died in the Tower in 1478 Richard was suspected of having a hand in his death, although the charge remains unproven as do so many others brought against him.

Edward IV's death made Richard Lord High Protector of the Realm for his nephew. The circumstances whereby he replaced that nephew as king have already been told. Richard and Anne were crowned at Westminster Abbey on 6 July 1483.

Richard was a small, slightly built man in contrast to his brother. He had one shoulder slightly higher than the other, but was far from being the malformed hunchback described by the Tudor propagandists. His portraits, all of one type, reveal a not unpleasant face with a rather worried expression. Richard showed every sign of being a competent ruler, but was never destined to prove his worth

The king and queen suffered a great blow on 9 April 1484 when their only child, Edward, Prince of Wales, who had always been sickly, died at Middleham Castle in Yorkshire. Queen Anne, always in poor health herself, never recovered from the shock and died at the Palace of Westminster on 16 March 1485, aged 28. She was buried in Westminster Abbey and in recent years the Richard III Society commissioned a wall plaque in her memory to be affixed near the site of her tomb.

Richard nominated his nephew John de la Pole, Earl of Lincoln, as heir presumptive, but the Lancastrians had found a new champion in the person of Henry Tudor, whose claim to the throne was tenuous to say the least. Henry landed at Milford Haven in August 1485 and travelled through Wales gaining support. Richard was in the north, but marched to Leicester with his army. The two armies met at Bosworth Field on 22 August. The king's army was twice the size of Henry's, but the turning point of the battle came when Lord Stanley (Henry's stepfather) and his 7,000 men deserted Richard and went over to Henry. Richard fought bravely to the last, but was finally cut down. The crest crown from his helmet fell off and rolled under a thorn bush, whence Stanley retrieved it and placed it on the head of Henry Tudor.

Richard's body, stripped of its armour, was laid across the back of a packhorse and taken back into Leicester, where it was buried in Grey Friars Abbey. At the Dissolution, his bones were dug up and thrown into the River Soar. He now has a monument in Leicester Cathedral, placed there by the Richard III Society.

THE TUDORS

Edward VI

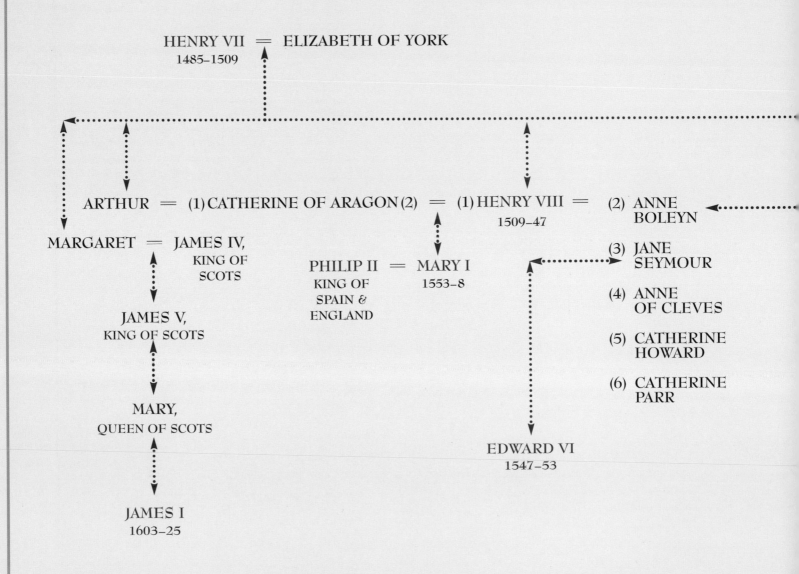

HENRY VII = ELIZABETH OF YORK
1485–1509

ARTHUR = (1) CATHERINE OF ARAGON (2) = (1) HENRY VIII = (2) ANNE
                                                1509–47   BOLEYN

MARGARET = JAMES IV,   (3) JANE
                    KING OF   PHILIP II = MARY I   SEYMOUR
                    SCOTS   KING OF   1553–8
                                   SPAIN &   (4) ANNE
JAMES V,   ENGLAND   OF CLEVES
KING OF SCOTS
                                                            (5) CATHERINE
                                                                HOWARD

MARY,   (6) CATHERINE
QUEEN OF SCOTS   PARR

                                          EDWARD VI
                                          1547–53

JAMES I
1603–25

43. Lady Margaret Beaufort, Countess of Richmond and Derby, the mother of Henry VII and the founder of Christ's and St John's Colleges, Cambridge, a lady of great piety and learning.

HENRY VII
1485–1509

Henry Tudor was the only child of Edmund Tudor, Earl of Richmond (one of the half-brothers of Henry VI), and his wife Lady Margaret Beaufort, in her turn the only child of John Beaufort, Duke of Somerset (grandson of John of Gaunt, Duke of Lancaster, the fourth son of Edward III). He was born to his 13-year-old mother at Pembroke Castle on 28 January 1457, nearly three months after the death of his father, whom he succeeded as Earl of Richmond at birth.

The infant Henry and his mother lived under the protection of his uncle Jasper Tudor, son of Henry V's widow Catherine and Owen Tudor. As Constable for the Lancastrians Tudor held Pembroke Castle until it was captured for the Yorkists by Lord Herbert in 1461. The change of ownership made little difference to Henry's life, Lord and Lady Herbert being kind foster-parents. Henry's mother remarried twice, first to Henry Stafford, who died in 1471, then to Thomas, Lord Stanley, but her early motherhood had rendered her incapable of bearing further children.

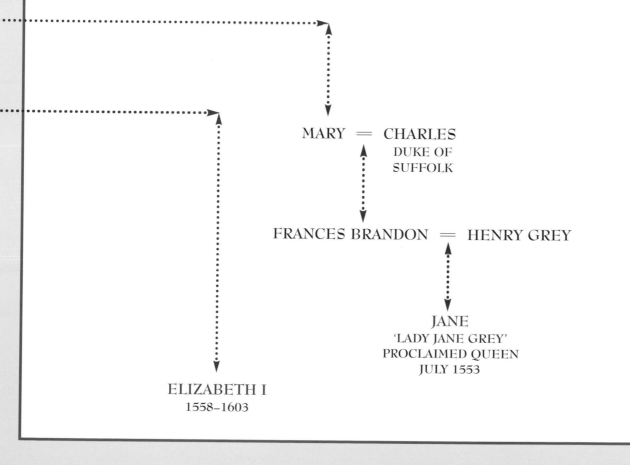

MARY = CHARLES
DUKE OF
SUFFOLK

FRANCES BRANDON = HENRY GREY

JANE
'LADY JANE GREY'
PROCLAIMED QUEEN
JULY 1553

ELIZABETH I
1558–1603

44. Henry VII, a contemporary portrait by an unknown artist, 1505.
The king's parsimony and shrewdness are apparent in this likeness.

The 'readeption' of Henry VI in 1470 brought Jasper Tudor back to Pembroke to fetch his nephew to court and there is a tradition that Henry attended his royal half-uncle's foundation at Eton. If so, it could only have been for a very short time as he returned to Wales with Jasper in 1471. After the Lancastrian defeats at Barnet and Tewkesbury, Pembroke Castle was besieged, but the Tudors, uncle and nephew, were helped to escape and sailed from Tenby en route for France. Stormy weather drove them ashore in Brittany, where they were hospitably received by the duke. They remained in Brittany for 13 years, successfully evading all attempts to extradite them.

Henry's path to the throne has already been related under Richard III. Genealogically, his claim was very tenuous as he descended from John of Gaunt's third marriage to Catherine Swynford, which had taken place after the birth of their children. These were subsequently legitimised but their ineligibility for succession to the throne was later added to the Act of Legitimisation.

Immediately after the victory of Bosworth Field, Henry proceeded to London and was crowned at Westminster Abbey on 30 October 1485. The following month Parliament passed an act confirming Henry's right to the throne and settling it on his legitimate issue. He was further petitioned by the Lords and Commons to marry Elizabeth of York, the eldest daughter of Edward IV, which he did at Westminster on 18 January 1486. The new queen became pregnant almost at once, so her coronation was deferred until 25 November 1487.

Apart from considering himself the lawful heir of the House of Lancaster and being married to the lawful heiress of the House of York, Henry also laid claim to a much older tradition. Through his Welsh grandfather he traced his descent from ancient British kings and saw himself as the lawful successor of the legendary King Arthur. He gave the name of Arthur to his first-born son and adopted the red dragon of Wales as one of the supporters of the royal arms.

Henry had to contend with two pretenders to the throne: Lambert Simnel, who claimed to be Edward, Earl of Warwick, the son of George, Duke of Clarence; and Perkin Warbeck, who pretended to be Richard, Duke of York, the younger son of Edward IV. Both were dealt with satisfactorily: the former was pardoned and lived for many years working as a turnspit in the royal kitchens; the latter was imprisoned in the Tower and eventually hanged after an attempted escape.

Henry brought peace and prosperity to the country after years of civil strife. He was parsimonious by nature, but maintained a splendid court and spent lavishly on building projects, rebuilding Baynard's Castle and Greenwich Palace, building a new palace at Richmond upon Thames to replace the old Sheen Palace, and adding the exquisite Lady Chapel, which has come to be known as Henry VII's Chapel, to Westminster Abbey. He also founded several religious houses and supported his mother's religious and educational foundations.

Henry arranged a grand royal marriage for his eldest son Arthur, Prince of Wales, with the Infanta Catherine of Aragon, the youngest daughter of the Spanish sovereigns Fernando II of Aragon and Isabel of Castile. It took place at St Paul's Cathedral on 14 November 1501, but in the following year Arthur fell ill with 'the sweating sickness' and died at Ludlow Castle on 2 April, leaving Catherine a childless widow. His death was a great blow to his parents and Queen Elizabeth herself died in childbirth at the Tower of London on her 37th birthday, 11 February 1503.

Henry contemplated remarrying from time to time, but never actually did so. His own health was poor and he suffered from gout and asthma. He died at Richmond Palace on 21 April 1509, aged 52. His mother survived him until June, when she died at the age of 66.

Henry was entombed with Elizabeth in his own chapel at Westminster beneath the magnificent bronze monument designed by Pietro Torrigiano. Henry's portrait by an unknown artist in the National Portrait Gallery was painted in 1505. It is a revealing likeness. His lean Welsh face peers out through shrewd blue-grey eyes, while his thin-lipped mouth speaks of his parsimony. Henry's later coins were the first to carry a portrait of the monarch that is more than just a stylised representation of a king.

HENRY VIII
1509–47

Henry, the second son and third child of Henry VII and Elizabeth of York, was born at Greenwich Palace on 28 June 1491. He was created Duke of York at the age of three in 1494 and at the age of ten played a prominent role in the marriage ceremonies of his brother Arthur, Prince of Wales, and Catherine of Aragon. Five months later, on Arthur's death, Henry became heir apparent and on 18 February 1503 his patent as Duke of York was cancelled and he was created Prince of Wales and Earl of Chester.

Henry received a good education, being well grounded in the classics by some of the leading scholars of the day. He was also a good linguist and a talented musician and when he succeeded his father in April 1509 he was regarded as the most accomplished prince of the age. Handsome and athletic, he bore a strong resemblance to his maternal grandfather, Edward IV, in person as well as in character.

One of the first acts of the new king was to marry his widowed sister-in-law, Catherine of Aragon. The marriage took place at Grey Friars Church, Greenwich, on 11 June 1509, the necessary papal dispensation being first obtained

45. Elizabeth of York, a late copy of the only known portrait type of this queen, which makes her look bland and lacking in character.

on the grounds that Catherine's marriage to Arthur had not been consummated. The royal couple proceeded to the Tower of London and thence to Westminster Abbey for their coronation on 24 June.

Three years after his accession Henry reopened the war with France and won the battle of the Spurs with the aid of Austrian mercenaries. The Scots took advantage of his absence abroad to invade England, where Catherine ruled as Regent, but were soundly beaten at Flodden Field, where Henry's brother-in-law, James IV (the husband of his sister Margaret), and the 'flower of the Scots nobility' were slain on 9 September 1513.

The next few years saw the rise of Thomas Wolsey, the son of an Ipswich butcher. He was appointed Almoner to the king in 1509, Canon of Windsor, Registrar of the Order of the Garter and a Privy Councillor in 1511, Archbishop of York in 1514, and in 1515 he received the Cardinal's hat from Pope Leo X. He became all-powerful and Henry relied on him for everything.

In 1520 Henry, who considered himself no mean theologian, published a book, *Assertio Septem Sacramentorum (The Defence of the Seven Sacraments)*, to refute the heresies of Martin Luther, which were beginning to gain ground on the Continent. The book was presented to the Pope, who rewarded the king with the new title Fidei Defensor (Defender of the Faith), which has been borne by all Henry's successors to the present day, regardless of the religious changes that have taken place.

Henry's marriage to Catherine had produced six children, but only one sickly girl, Mary, had survived infancy. By the mid-1520s it became obvious that Catherine, who was five and a half years older than Henry, was unlikely at the age of 40 to bear any further children. Henry was desperate for a male heir and even considered making his illegitimate son Henry FitzRoy, Duke of Richmond, his heir, but the boy was also delicate, and Henry thought better of it. The only remedy was to dissolve his marriage to Catherine and marry again.

Henry was soon able to convince himself that his lack of a son was a sign of divine retribution for having married his sister-in-law, and instructed Wolsey to open negotiations with the Holy See to have his marriage annulled. Catherine fought the petition vigorously, backed by her nephew the Emperor Charles V. Wolsey's failure to procure the annulment from Rome after several years of protracted negotiation earned him the animosity of the king's paramour, Anne Boleyn, who was eager to become queen, and brought about his dismissal as Chancellor. A more far-reaching consequence of the whole business was the exasperated Henry's break with Rome, leading to the establishment of the Church of England.

In 1533 Henry nominated Thomas Cranmer as Archbishop of Canterbury and the appointment was confirmed by Rome. Cranmer begged the king to be allowed to decide Henry's 'great matter', as the divorce suit was called, and in May declared the marriage to Catherine null and void. Anne had become pregnant by the king in December 1532 and on 25 January 1533 Henry had jumped the gun and gone through a secret marriage ceremony with her, which was validated retrospectively by Cranmer's pronouncement.

Catherine had her daughter Mary taken from her in 1531 and was moved from place to place for fear of a popular uprising in her favour. After the annulment she was deprived of the title of Queen and styled Princess Dowager of Wales. She had the hollow satisfaction of knowing that the Pope had pronounced her marriage valid on 23 March 1534. She was last confined at Kimbolton Castle, Huntingdonshire, and died there of cancer on 7 January 1536. She was buried in Peterborough Cathedral.

Anne, who had supplanted Catherine, was the daughter of Sir Thomas Boleyn, later created Earl of Wiltshire and Earl of Ormonde, and his wife, Lady Elizabeth Howard, daughter of Thomas Howard, 2nd Duke of Norfolk. Her marriage to Henry was declared valid on 28 May 1533 and on 1 June she was crowned queen at Westminster Abbey, the last occasion on which a queen consort was crowned separately from her husband. On 7 September she gave birth to a daughter, much to Henry's chagrin.

Henry's Reformation Parliament confirmed his title as 'of the Church of England on Earth Supreme Head' and copies of the new English translation of the Bible were ordered to be placed in every church; but in all other respects, very little was altered, the Latin mass and other ceremonies being retained.

By 1536 Anne had been superseded in Henry's affections by one of her maids of honour, Jane Seymour, and when Anne was prematurely delivered of a stillborn son on 29 January 1536, her fate was sealed. She was arrested on 2 May and charged with adultery and with an incestuous relationship with her own brother. Found guilty and condemned to death on 15 May, her marriage was declared null and void by Cranmer two days later on account of the affinity between Anne and Henry created by his former relationship with her sister Mary. On 19 May 1536 Anne was beheaded on Tower Green by a swordsman brought from Calais. She was buried in the chapel of St Peter-ad-Vincula in the Tower.

The same year saw the commencement of the Dissolution of the Monasteries, which had become immensely rich and powerful. Henry was desperately in need of money and aided by his new Chancellor, Thomas Cromwell, saw the spoliation of the monasteries as an easy means of obtaining it.

Henry and Jane Seymour were married on 30 May 1536. She was over 30 and was the daughter of Sir John Seymour of Wolf Hall, Savernake, Wiltshire, and his wife, Margery Wentworth. Plans for her coronation were postponed because of an outbreak of plague in London and later deferred on account of Jane's pregnancy. On 12 October 1537 the queen gave birth to the long-awaited male heir. Twelve days later, on 24 October, she died of puerperal fever at Hampton Court Palace. She was buried in St George's Chapel, Windsor.

Henry remained a widower for over two years until a new marriage was negotiated for him by Cromwell. The bride was the 24-year-old Anne of Cleves, second daughter of John III, Duke of Cleves, and his wife Marie of Jülich. When Anne arrived in England, Henry found her face less attractive than her portrait by Holbein had led him to suppose, declaring her 'a Flanders mare', but he had to go through with the ceremony at Greenwich on 6 January 1540. Henry was careful not to consummate the marriage, and although the couple slept together in the same bed, Anne was so innocent that she knew no better. Henry got Convocation (Synod) to declare the marriage null and void on 9 July on the grounds of his own lack of consent and Anne's pre-contract with the son of the Duke of Lorraine. After the annulment Anne was very well treated by Henry, receiving an ample income and a household establishment befitting her rank. She often appeared at court as the king's 'beloved sister' and attended the coronation of Mary I, walking with Elizabeth in the coronation procession. She died at her house in Chelsea on 17 July 1557, and was buried in Westminster Abbey, the last survivor of Henry's six wives.

Thomas Cromwell fell into disgrace through his bungling of Henry's fourth marriage. He was arrested, charged with treason and heresy, and executed on 28 July, the day on which Henry married his fifth wife, Catherine Howard. The new queen was a first cousin of Anne Boleyn, being the daughter of Lord Edmund Howard (a brother of Anne's mother) and his first wife, Joyce, daughter of Sir Richard Culpeper. She was only 19 or 20 and lively, vivacious and pretty. The king was besotted with her and lavished lands and jewellery on her. Catherine had had lovers in the past, however, and it is hardly surprising that united to a husband some 30 years her senior and fast growing gross and repugnant, she took up with them again. An informer told the Council and it became Cranmer's task to tell the king of his wife's infidelity. After refusing to believe it at first, Henry indulged in an orgy of self-pity and then ordered Catherine to be removed from Hampton Court and placed under guard at Syon House. After her lovers had been brought to trial, found guilty and executed, a Bill of Attainder against the queen was brought into Parliament and received the royal assent (through a commission, in order to spare Henry's feelings) on 11 February 1542. Two days later the luckless Catherine shared the same fate as her cousin Anne Boleyn and was buried near her in the Chapel of St Peter-ad-Vincula.

The sordid affair made Henry an old man. He was a physical wreck, obese, prematurely senile and stinking from an ulcerated leg, generally accepted to be the result of syphilis, although some modern writers have denied this. He required a nurse rather than a wife and found both in the person of Catherine, Lady Latimer, whom he married at Hampton Court on 12 July 1543. Catherine, who was about 31, was the daughter of Sir Thomas Parr of Kendal,

46. *Catherine of Aragon, Henry VIII's first queen,*
a portrait painted about 1530, when she was
already over 40 and lengthy divorce
proceedings were in progress.

49. *An eighteenth-century engraving of Anne of Cleves,*
after Holbein's portrait.

47. *Anne Boleyn, by an unknown artist. The charm*
that captivated Henry is apparent in this portrait.

50. *A portrait after Holbein formerly identified as being of*
Catherine Howard, of whom there is no authentic likeness.
This sitter is obviously far older than the sprightly Catherine.

48. *Henry VIII's third queen, Jane Seymour,*
an engraving after Holbein.

51. *Catherine Parr, Henry VIII's sixth and last queen.*
This portrait has only recently been identified and was
previously believed to represent Lady Jane Grey.

52. Henry VIII, England's most easily recognisable king,
from a portrait by an unknown artist, painted about 1542.

Westmorland, and his wife Maud, daughter of Sir Thomas Green, of Green's Norton, Northamptonshire. She had been married and widowed twice, first to Sir Edward Borough (or Burgh), eldest son of Thomas, 3rd Lord Borough of Gainsborough, and secondly to John Neville, 3rd Lord Latimer, whom she had nursed devotedly through his final illness. She had no children by either husband.

Henry's sixth wife proved a good choice. At Christmas 1543 she brought together the king's three children, Mary, Elizabeth and Edward, all of whom had developed a genuine affection for her. In the following year she was appointed Governor of the Realm and Protector when the French war was renewed and Henry was absent from England for two months. Catherine's religious inclinations leant towards the reformers and a charge of heresy was drawn up against her by the pro-Roman faction at court. The queen managed to obtain a copy of the bill which had been drafted and cleverly persuaded Henry that she had talked theology with him only to ease his infirmity. He accepted her explanation and when a party arrived to arrest her and take her to the Tower he sent them packing, calling Wriothesley, one of her accusers, 'knave, arrant knave, beast and fool'.

Henry succumbed at last to his many ailments and died on 28 January 1547, aged only 55, but an old and worn-out man. He was buried with his beloved Jane Seymour in St George's Chapel, Windsor.

Henry VIII, the first English sovereign to be styled 'Majesty', has come to typify the English monarchy and his likeness is one that is instantly recognisable by most people. His love of learning was genuine. He founded Trinity College, Cambridge, and endowed five regius professorships at the university, redeploying some of the money gained through the Dissolution. He was also a builder and embellisher of palaces, Bridewell, Whitehall, St James's, Hampton Court (acquired from Cardinal Wolsey) and Nonsuch all being built or enlarged at his behest.

The widowed Queen Catherine was immediately courted by Thomas Seymour, Baron Seymour of Sudeley, a brother of the late Queen Jane. He had sought her hand after the death of her second husband, but the king had carried off the widow for himself. Seymour now renewed his suit with success and he and Catherine were married in April or May 1547. By the end of the year Catherine was pregnant for the first time at the age of 36. On 29 August 1548 she gave birth to a daughter at Sudeley Castle, but puerperal fever ensued and she died on 5 September, being buried in the chapel at Sudeley Castle. Her little daughter, Mary, appears to have died young, although there is no record of her death.

EDWARD VI
1547–53

The only son of Henry VIII by his third wife Jane Seymour was born at Hampton Court Palace on 12 October 1537. His mother died two weeks later and he was confided to the care of nurses until his stepmother Queen Catherine Parr took a hand in his upbringing and chose four of the greatest scholars in the kingdom to be his tutors. These men imparted not only a sound knowledge of Greek, Latin and English, but also the tenets of the Protestant Reformation that had swept through Germany and the Netherlands. As a result Edward was precocious beyond his years and something of a prig. The fact that he was always sickly and had no companions of his own age accentuated this.

Edward succeeded his father at the age of nine. The news of Henry's death was delayed for three days while the Council debated the fate of the Duke of Norfolk, who was under sentence of death in the Tower, and finally decided to spare him. Edward's maternal uncle Lord Hertford became Protector of the Realm and was created Duke of Somerset, and the young king was crowned at Westminster Abbey on 20 February 1547. John Knox, Ridley, Latimer and Hooper, all zealous reformers, were appointed court chaplains and Archbishop Cranmer was charged with compiling the first English Prayer Book, which appeared in 1548.

Early in 1549 Edward was forced to agree to the execution of his favourite uncle, Thomas Seymour, Catherine Parr's widower, who had been convicted for high treason. This served to embitter Edward towards his other uncle, the Protector Somerset, whose own fall and subsequent execution he viewed with a show of indifference. Somerset was replaced as Protector by John Dudley, Earl of Warwick, who was created Duke of Northumberland.

53. Edward VI, a 'swagger portrait' of the boy king by an unknown artist.

Edward's love of learning caused him to found numerous grammar schools which bore his name. He gave the old palace of Bridewell to the corporation of London to provide a workhouse (and eventually a lunatic asylum), and converted Grey Friars Monastery into Christ's Hospital.

The young king was plagued with ill-health, possibly congenital syphilis inherited from his father. In 1552 he was said to have suffered from measles and then from smallpox, both doubtful diagnoses. Early in the following year it became apparent that he was suffering from pulmonary tuberculosis. This was accompanied by many distressing additional symptoms and after great suffering Edward died at Greenwich Palace on 6 July 1553, aged 15. He was buried near the tomb of his grandfather Henry VII in Westminster Abbey, but has no memorial.

JANE
10–19 July 1553

While Edward VI lay dying, the Protector Northumberland, knowing and fearing the Catholic reaction which would come about under Mary, induced the king to nominate Lady Jane Grey, the granddaughter of Henry VIII's sister Mary, as heiress-presumptive on 21 June 1553. This excluded not only the king's half-sisters Mary and Elizabeth and the descendants of his aunt Margaret, Queen of Scots, but also Lady Jane's own mother, Frances, Duchess of Suffolk.

Lady Jane was the second, but eldest surviving, daughter of Henry Grey, Duke of Suffolk and Marquess of Dorset, and his wife Lady Frances Brandon, eldest daughter and co-heiress of Charles Brandon, Duke of Suffolk, and his wife Mary, Queen Dowager of France, third daughter of Henry VII. She was born at Bradgate, Leicestershire, in October 1537, the same month as the king she was to succeed, and like him was extremely well educated, being learned in Hebrew, Greek and Latin. She was also staunchly Protestant.

On 21 May 1553, the wily Northumberland had arranged Jane's marriage to his sixth son, Lord Guilford Dudley, a callow youth of 16 or 17, the ceremony taking place at Durham House, London. Jane was very reluctant to accept the crown forced upon her by her

54. The 'Nine Days Queen', Lady Jane Grey, a nineteenth-century engraving after a painting by Robert Smirke, RA, of this tragic girl being persuaded to accept the crown.

ambitious father-in-law, but was publicly proclaimed queen after the news of Edward's death on 10 July 1553. She made her state entry into the Tower of London with much pomp, wearing specially raised shoes to give her height, and with her long train supported by her mother.

Jane showed some spirit by adamantly refusing the suggestion that her husband, for whom at that time she had little affection, should be proclaimed king with her. Whether or not she would have remained unyielding on this point is academic, for her reign only lasted nine days and she was deposed on 19 July 1553. The nobility had been incensed by Northumberland's presumption and the majority of the people, too, wanted Mary, not Jane, as queen.

Northumberland's army was dispersed without bloodshed and he was condemned and beheaded on Tower Hill on 22 August 1553. Jane and Guilford were arraigned, convicted of high treason and confined to the Tower. They were the innocent victims of the overwhelming ambition of their parents and it was only with reluctance and after much heart-searching that Mary I agreed to their execution.

The young couple had drawn closer to each other in their adversity and as Guilford walked to his death on Tower Hill on the morning of 12 February 1554, Jane bade him farewell from her prison window. A little later she saw his headless body being returned in a cart with his head wrapped in a cloth. She was granted a more private execution on Tower Green on the same day and met her end with calm fortitude. The pair were buried in the Chapel of St Peter-ad-Vincula.

55. A portrait of Mary I by Master John, 1544, showing her at the age of 28, when she was still a princess.

MARY I AND PHILIP OF SPAIN
1553–8   *1554–8*

Mary was the second daughter and fifth child born to Henry VIII by Catherine of Aragon, her birth having been preceded by those of a stillborn daughter, two short-lived sons and a stillborn son. She saw the light of day at Greenwich Palace on 18 February 1516. Her father's disappointment at her being a girl was tempered by his hope of further male issue to come, but Catherine's sixth and last pregnancy produced another stillborn daughter.

Making the best of it for the time being, Henry gave Mary her own court at Ludlow Castle and she enjoyed many of the prerogatives usually given to a Prince of Wales. The Countess of Salisbury was appointed her governess and she studied Greek, Latin, French, Italian, science and music. She was a sickly child, suffering from severe headaches and defective eyesight, probably a result of the congenital syphilis which Henry is believed to have bestowed on his off-spring.

*56. Electrotype of a Renaissance medal of Mary I and Philip of Spain,
after an original by Jacopo da Trezzo, dated c.1555.*

Apart from her chronic ill-health, Mary's childhood and young womanhood were made wretched by the protracted divorce proceedings of her parents and the degradations and humiliations to which she and her mother were subjected. In 1533 she was declared illegitimate and sent to Hatfield to live with her infant half-sister Elizabeth under the care of Anne Boleyn's aunt Lady Shelton. It speaks well for her character that she was able to feel some genuine sisterly feeling towards the child of the woman who had replaced her mother.

After Anne Boleyn's execution, Mary was recalled to court and reconciled with her father after being induced to acknowledge the fact that her mother's marriage to him had been unlawful and that she herself was, therefore, illegitimate. She also acknowledged the king as head of the church. In 1537 she stood godmother to her half-brother Edward and acted as chief mourner at the funeral of her stepmother Queen Jane Seymour.

Catherine Parr's influence drew the royal family closer together and Mary was reinstated in the line of succession to the throne. In 1549 she refused to comply with the Act of Uniformity requiring the use of Cranmer's new Prayer Book, and continued to have the Latin mass celebrated in her household. This intransigence on her part resulted in the abortive attempt to divert the succession to Lady Jane Grey on Edward VI's death.

When the young king died Mary was staying at Framlingham Castle, Suffolk, and learning that the country was for her rather than for Jane, set out for London, where she made a triumphal entry in the company of her half-sister, Elizabeth. All support for Jane collapsed and Mary's succession was unchallenged. She at once ordered the release of the Duke of Norfolk and Stephen Gardiner from the Tower, restoring the latter to the see of Winchester and making him Chancellor. It was Gardiner who crowned Mary at Westminster Abbey on 1 October 1553.

Mary set about singlemindedly to restore the old order, the Latin mass and papal supremacy. Her first Parliament abolished Edward VI's religious laws and reasserted her own legitimacy. She was already 37 and saw the necessity of marrying as soon as possible in order to provide an heir to the throne other than Elizabeth, whose religious leanings were doubtful. After rejecting the Earl of Devon, she determined on marrying the heir to the Spanish throne, Philip, son of her first cousin the Emperor Charles V. The Commons, backed by Gardiner, begged her to reconsider, fearing the threat to English independence, but she was adamant and her persistence let to a rebellion headed by Sir Thomas Wyatt, who marched on London but was speedily defeated and executed. The queen and Philip were married at Winchester Cathedral on 25 July 1554. At Mary's insistence Philip received the title of king and all official documents and Acts of Parliament were dated in their joint names. His head, facing that of his wife, also appeared on the coinage.

Philip is the only consort of a reigning queen of England to have enjoyed the crown matrimonial as king consort and in his wife's eyes, at least, co-regent. He was born at Valladolid in Spain on 21 April 1527, so was Mary's junior by 11 years. He had already been married to Maria of Portugal, by whom he had one son, and had been a widower since 1545. Mary fell in love with him with all the ardour of a young girl, but he found her physically repellant and after 14 months of marriage made an excuse to return to Spain, leaving Mary deluding herself with a false pregnancy.

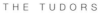

Mary's vigorous attempts to eradicate Protestantism resulted in the so-called 'Marian Persecutions' in which some 300 Protestants, including Cranmer, Ridley, Latimer and Hooper, suffered death for their faith. This has earned Mary the unjust epithet of 'Bloody Mary'. She was not naturally a cruel woman, albeit a bigoted one, and possessed a measure of her father's greatness with which, had she been blessed with good health, she might well have achieved her aim to restore England to papal obedience. It has to be stated that the number of Protestants who suffered death or persecution under Mary was more than balanced by the number of Catholics who were to suffer under Elizabeth.

In 1557, to Mary's great joy, Philip returned to England and persuaded Mary to join Spain in war with France. As a result, England's last remaining continental possession, Calais, was lost. Philip left in July, never to return, and Mary said that when she was dead the words 'Philip' and 'Calais' would be found engraved on her heart.

The queen had come to rely very heavily on her kinsman Cardinal Pole, who had succeeded Cranmer as Archbishop of Canterbury in 1556 and acted as the papal legate for the reconciliation of the Church of England to Rome. In November 1558 both Mary and

57. Elizabeth I in her coronation robes, by an unknown artist.

Pole fell ill with influenza. She died at St James's Palace on 17 November and he at Lambeth Palace on the following day. She was buried in Westminster Abbey. Philip was to remarry twice and died in the great monastery palace of El Escorial, which he had built, on 13 September 1598.

ELIZABETH I
1558–1603

The only daughter of Henry VIII and Anne Boleyn was born at Greenwich Palace on 7 September 1533. Her father was so confident that the baby would be a boy that the documents announcing the birth for despatch to foreign courts had already been prepared and there was only enough room to add one final 's' to the word 'prince'. Nevertheless, Elizabeth was proclaimed heiress presumptive to the crown, replacing her half-sister Mary. Fortunately, she was a strong, healthy child.

After Anne Boleyn's disgrace and execution, Elizabeth was declared illegitimate by Act of Parliament and deprived of her place in the succession. She was sent to live away from court and was very ill-provided for until her last step-mother, Queen Catherine Parr, reunited the royal family again. Elizabeth shared her half brother Edward's tutors and was reinstated in the order of succession.

In July 1553 Elizabeth entered London with her half-sister Mary and later attended Mary's coronation, accompanied by Anne of Cleves. In the following year she refused to have any part in Sir Thomas Wyatt's rebellion, but was nevertheless, at Gardiner's instigation, imprisoned in the Tower of London, protesting her innocence. She was never brought to trial and was later removed to Woodstock and thence to Hatfield, Hertfordshire, where according to tradition she was sitting reading beneath a tree in the grounds (rather unlikely in the middle of November, it might be thought) when news was brought of Mary's death and her own accession to the throne.

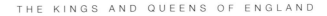

58. An allegorical portrait of Elizabeth I standing on a map of England, painted by Marcus Gheeraerts the Younger in about 1592.

Elizabeth was crowned at Westminster Abbey on 15 January 1559. The see of Canterbury was vacant and the only bishop who could be found to perform the ceremony was Owen Oglethorpe, Bishop of Carlisle. Elizabeth expressed her displeasure at some of the more Catholic aspects of the rite, making plain her leanings towards Protestantism and her determination not to pursue the reconciliation with the Holy See undertaken by Mary. It was not until 1570, however, that Pope Pius V excommunicated her and absolved her subjects of their allegiance to her – by then a very empty gesture.

Elizabeth's reign is considered a golden age in English history, although it was not without its moments of controversy, including repeated clashes with Spain and dissension within her own court. One deed that reflected poorly upon her was the execution of her cousin Mary, Queen of Scots, in 1587 after 18 years of captivity as a political prisoner in England. In Elizabeth's defence it must be said that Mary did represent a threat and was the hope of the Catholic party forever intriguing on her behalf with a view to kill Elizabeth and set Mary on the throne. It was only with the greatest reluctance that Elizabeth signed Mary's death warrant and when news of the execution reached her 'she gave herself over to grief, putting herself into mourning weeds and shedding abundance of tears'.

Drake's defeat of the Spanish Armada in the following year was the crowning glory of the reign and consolidated Elizabeth's position as one of the strongest monarchs in Europe. The victory was made possible by the maritime experience of English seamen, whom the queen had encouraged to seek new wealth overseas. The Elizabethan Age was one of adventure and discovery, Hawkins, Drake, Raleigh and the Gilberts all extending England's possessions in the Americas The colony of Virginia was founded and named after the 'Virgin Queen' and the East India Company also came into being. Elizabeth herself never left the country, but made many royal progresses throughout England so that places where she is reputed to have slept are legion. Literature flourished, too, under Elizabeth and Shakespeare, Spenser, Sidney, Bacon, Marlowe and many others gave her reign a rare distinction.

Elizabeth was vain and loved to dress richly with many jewels. She refused to admit to ageing; in later life she wore a huge red wig over her thinning hair and employed cosmetics to achieve a dead white complexion, which would appear grotesque today. She also loved dancing and the company of young men, who flattered her and dubbed her 'Gloriana'.

Elizabeth saw early in her reign that her strength lay in her single state and cleverly juggled her many suitors from home and abroad (among them the French heir presumptive the Duke of Alençon, Henry of Navarre, and her former brother-in-law Philip II of Spain) until she was well past middle age. Glorying in her image as the semi-divine Virgin Queen, Elizabeth often declared England to be her only spouse.

59. *Mary, Queen of Scots, after Nicholas Hilliard,*
c.1610. As Elizabeth I's potential rival,
she was beheaded in 1587. Her son
eventually succeeded Elizabeth.

60. *Robert Dudley, Ist Earl of Leicester*
(c.1532–1588), Elizabeth I's great favourite
and one-time suitor, c.1575.

She summoned Parliament only 13 times in 44 years, but she was well served by her advisers, the Cecils, Sir Nicholas Bacon and Francis Walsingham, and was a loyal mistress to those who served her loyally. She could be scathing with those who displeased her, however, and towards the end of her life exhibited a parsimony akin to that of her grandfather Henry VII

If Elizabeth had a weakness, it was her partiality for unworthy but handsome young male favourites such as Robert Dudley, Earl of Leicester, and Robert Devereux, Earl of Essex, provoking much scandalous speculation. Sir Walter Raleigh was another but more worthy favourite who lost the queen's regard after he had the temerity to marry one of her maids of honour without seeking her permission.

Elizabeth's health was generally good throughout her life. In January 1603 she was suffering from a cold when she moved from Whitehall to Richmond Palace. She recovered, but fell ill again at the end of February with severe tonsillitis, temporarily relieved when a small abscess broke. She became very ill again on 18 March, but refused to go to bed, lying instead on a heap of cushions piled on the floor. In a last flash of her great spirit, when told by Cecil that she must go to bed, she replied, 'Little man, little man, "must" is not a word to use to princes.' Elizabeth died at three o'clock in the morning on 24 March 1603. She had signified her assent that the King of Scots, son of the beheaded Mary, should be her successor and a messenger at once set out for Scotland to convey the news of his accession to him.

Elizabeth was buried in Westminster Abbey in the same vault as her half-sister, Mary I. The tomb erected above it bears Elizabeth's effigy only, but the Latin epitaph translates, 'Consorts both in Throne and Grave, here rest we two sisters, Elizabeth and Mary, in hope of our resurrection.'

61. *Robert Devereux, 2nd Earl of Essex*
(1566–1601), Elizabeth I's last favourite,
who fell from favour after his failure as
governor-general of Ireland and was
eventually beheaded as a traitor.

JAMES I = ANNE OF DENMARK
KING OF SCOTS
1567–1625
KING OF ENGLAND
1603–25

ELIZABETH STUART = FREDERICK V
OF BOHEMIA

HENRY FREDERICK
PRINCE OF WALES

SOPHIA = ERNEST
ELECTOR OF
HANOVER

WILLIAM OF NASSAU = MARY
PRINCE OF ORANGE

GEORGE I
1714–27

WILLIAM III = MARY II
1689–1702   1689–94

62. Henry Frederick, Prince of Wales, by Robert Peake,
c.1610. The eldest son of James I and a young man of great
promise, he died of typhoid at an early age.

THE STUARTS

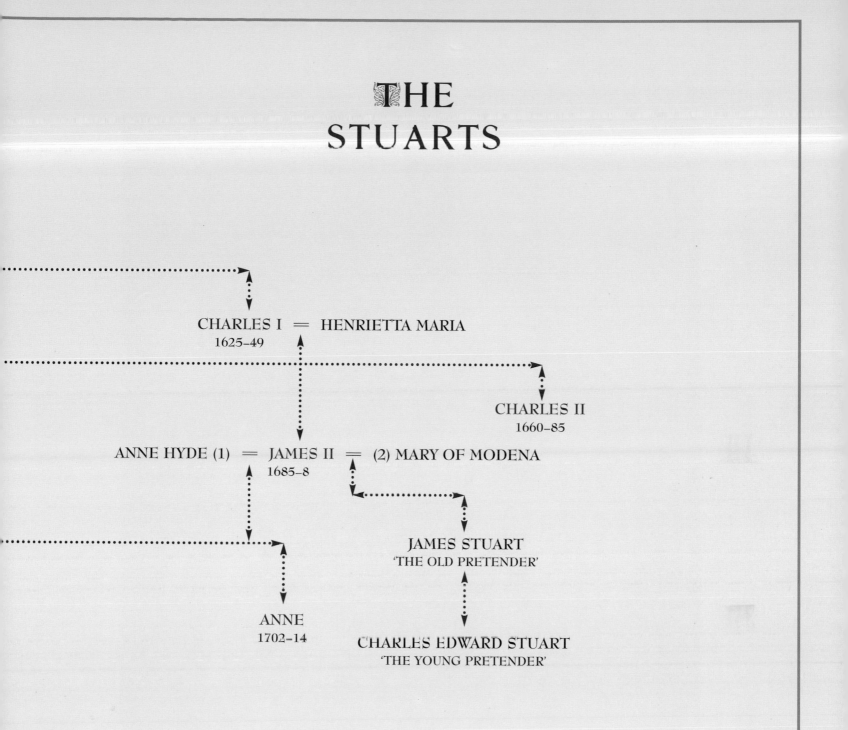

CHARLES I = HENRIETTA MARIA
1625–49

CHARLES II
1660–85

ANNE HYDE (1) = JAMES II = (2) MARY OF MODENA
1685–8

JAMES STUART
'THE OLD PRETENDER'

ANNE
1702–14

CHARLES EDWARD STUART
'THE YOUNG PRETENDER'

JAMES I
1603–25

The only son of Mary, Queen of Scots, and her second husband, Henry Stuart, Lord Darnley, was born at Edinburgh Castle on 19 June 1566 and named Charles James, the first name being in honour of his godfather, King Charles IX of France, the brother of Mary's first husband. He was the first British sovereign to bear more than one Christian name. Both his parents were grandchildren of Henry VII's daughter Margaret Tudor, who had married James IV, King of Scots, and, after his death at Flodden, Archibald Douglas, 6th Earl of Angus.

As heir apparent James bore the titles of Duke of Rothesay and Prince and Steward of Scotland from birth. He was only eight months old when his father was murdered at Kirk o' Field on 10 February 1567. Mary's suspected involvement in the death and her subsequent marriage on 15 May to James Hepburn, Earl of Bothwell, led to her forced abdication on 24 July and James's proclamation as James VI. Five days later, although only one year and one month old, he was solemnly crowned at Stirling.

63. James I of England (VI of Scotland), by Daniel Mytens, 1621. The king is
magnificently portrayed in his Garter robes.

James was placed under the guardianship of the Earl of Mar and later of Sir Alexander Erskine and received a sound education from the historian and poet George Buchanan. Through-out his reign in Scotland he was controlled by powerful nobles and the extreme Protestant clergy of the Kirk, and was little more than a pawn in their political machinations.

In a series of ceremonies, culminating at Kronborg on 21 January 1590, James was married to Anne, the second daughter of King Frederick II of Denmark and Sophia of Mecklenburg-Güstrow, who had been born at Skanderborg Castle in Jutland on 14 October 1574. She was a plain, characterless and rather masculine girl and made an ideal consort for James, who had grown up with little female company and tended to focus his affections on members of his own sex.

The couple returned to Scotland in leisurely fashion, landing at Leith on 1 May, and Anne's coronation in the chapel of Holyrood House followed on 17 May. In the course of the next twelve years she gave birth to five children, three of whom, Henry, Elizabeth and Charles, survived infancy.

As soon as James received the news of Elizabeth's death he set out for London, unaccompanied by Anne, who was nearing the end of her sixth pregnancy. After she had been delivered of a stillborn son, she set out to join him and they were crowned together at Westminster Abbey on 25 July 1603.

Having escaped from the control of the Scottish lords and clergy, James was determined to exert his authority as ruler in his new kingdom. He propounded the theory of 'the divine right of kings', maintaining that the king was above the law and answerable only to God. He was a shrewd enough statesman not to press his claims too far and when Parliament consistently refused to vote him extra funds, turned to other ways of raising money. In 1611 he instituted the order of baronets, a new hereditary honour between knighthood and the peerage, and sold the dignity for £1,080.

In 1605 an attempt by Catholic sympathisers to blow up the king and Parliament at its state opening on 5 November was discovered and the conspirators were rounded up and duly executed. James was terrified by the conspiracy and for

64. *Anne of Denmark, James I's queen, here portrayed in mourning for her son Henry, Prince of Wales, c.1612.*

many days thereafter refused to leave his apartments, allowing only trusted fellow-Scots to attend him. A new wave of anti-Catholic feeling ensued and the extreme Puritans pushed for further religious reforms, including the abolition of bishops, which James stoutly opposed, stating, 'No Bishop, no King'.

Queen Anne had given birth to two more daughters after coming to England, but both died in infancy. They have charming monuments in Westminster Abbey. James's eldest son, Henry Frederick, Prince of Wales, was a handsome young man of great promise, but he died of typhoid on 6 November 1612, aged 18. Four months later his sister Elizabeth was married to Frederick V, Elector Palatine and for one winter King of Bohemia. Through their youngest daughter, she was destined to become the ancestor of Britain's Hanoverian sovereigns.

Queen Anne died at Hampton Court Palace on 4 March 1619, and was buried in Westminster Abbey. James was little moved by her death, his affections by then being entirely centred on George Villiers, a young man he had first met in 1614 and advanced from honour to honour, culminating in the dukedom of Buckingham in 1623. James affectionately nicknamed him 'Steenie' from a fancied resemblance to the figure in a painting of the martyrdom of St Stephen.

65. Elizabeth, Queen of Bohemia, in a portrait from the studio of Michael Jansz. van Miereveldt, c.1623.
The daughter of James I, Elizabeth had a life that saw many vicissitudes.
Her grandson, through her youngest daughter, eventually became George I.

66. Charles I, by Daniel Mytens, 1631.

67. Henrietta Maria, Charles I's French queen, in a portrait after Sir Anthony van Dyck, c.1632–5.

James was unattractive in appearance, a large head with rheumy eyes topping an ungainly and ill-proportioned body with bow legs. He suffered from the 'royal malady' of porphyria, as had his mother, and in addition was coarse, ill-mannered and a physical and moral coward. He was, however, naturally able and intelligent. The Spanish ambassador called him 'the wisest fool in Christendom'. James was the author of several books and treatises and commissioned the 'King James Bible', which remained the standard version of the Bible in English for centuries to come.

James's final illness began early in 1625. Kidney failure and a stroke were the probable causes of his death, which took place at Theobald's Park, Hertfordshire, on 27 March 1625. He was buried in Westminster Abbey.

CHARLES I
1625–49

Charles, the second son of James I and Anne of Denmark, was born at Dunfermline on 19 November 1600. He was a delicate child, still unable to walk or talk at the age of three, and was left behind in the care of nurses and servants when his parents went to London with his elder brother and sister on his father's accession to the English throne. He finally made the journey in July 1604 and was placed in the charge of Lady Carey, whose husband had carried the news of James's accession to Scotland. Under her patient care he gradually learned to walk on his rickety legs and talk with his stammering tongue.

Charles adored his elder brother Henry and longed to emulate him; when Henry died Charles felt it keenly. The separation from his sister Elizabeth on her marriage in 1613 was another blow and Charles virtually became an only child.

Charles was created Duke of Albany in the peerage of Scotland in 1603 and Duke of York in the peerage of England in 1605. He was further created Prince of Wales and Earl of Chester in November 1616.

Even as an adult Charles was only five feet four inches tall, with a long, mournful countenance and heavy-lidded eyes. He bore himself with great dignity, however, and his father planned a marriage for him with the Infanta Maria of Spain. In 1623 he was sent to Madrid accompanied by 'Steenie' to pay court to her. They travelled via Paris, where Charles had a first sighting of the French king's sister Henrietta Maria, who was eventually to become his bride. Charles and Buckingham were well received at the Spanish court, but the marriage negotiations foundered on the stumbling block of religion and the pair returned to England in October.

Charles succeeded his father in March 1625 and on 1 May was married by proxy at Paris to Henrietta Maria, the youngest daughter of King Henry IV of France and his second wife, Marie de' Medici. She was his junior by nine years, having been born at the Hôtel du Louvre, Paris, on 26 November 1609. On her arrival in England the marriage was solemnised at Canterbury on 13 June 1625.

Charles was crowned at Westminster Abbey on 2 February 1626, but because of the religious difficulties his queen was not crowned with him. The early years of the marriage were uneasy, but eventually the young couple developed a close relationship which was to ripen into a deep and abiding love. Nine children were born to them between 1629 and 1644, three sons and three daughters surviving infancy.

Charles encountered the same troubles with Parliament as his father and clashed with its members over a combination of financial, religious and political issues. After summoning and dissolving it three times, the king decided to

68. The five children of Charles I in 1637, after Van Dyck. The future Charles II is in the centre.

69. A contemporary German print depicting the beheading of Charles I
outside the Banqueting House in Whitehall on 30 January 1649.

govern without it and in 1629 began 11 years of personal rule. To raise revenue he sold monopolies and levied the unpopular 'ship money' from seaports and later from inland towns. After Parliament had been summoned again in 1640, Charles proved unable to resist demands for the execution of his adviser Thomas Wentworth, Earl of Strafford, and reconciliation between the king and Parliament became impossible. Matters came to a head on 4 January 1642, when Charles committed the unprecedented act of entering the House of Commons with an armed guard to demand the arrest of five members of Parliament, who were planning the impeachment of the queen. Forewarned, they had already made their escape. In the face of public hostility, Charles fled from London and civil war became inevitable.

The king raised his standard at Nottingham and the long struggle between Cavaliers (the Royalists) and Roundheads (the Parliamentarians) began in earnest. The opening battle of Edgehill on 23 October 1642 was indecisive, but throughout 1643 the tide of war seemed to be running largely with the Royalists. Subsequently, however, they were to suffer crippling defeats at the hands of Oliver Cromwell's New Model Army, culminating in the disasters of Marston Moor in 1644 and Naseby in 1645. Charles surrendered to the Scots in 1646, expecting to be well treated, but was promptly handed over to the English Parliamentarians and confined at Carisbrooke Castle on the Isle of Wight. From there he was brought to trial in Westminster Hall before a tribunal of 135 judges. Refusing to recognise the legality of a court that could try a king, Charles declined to plead and was found guilty by 68 votes to 67, a majority of only one. Sentence of death was passed on him and on 30 January 1649 he walked from St James's Palace, where he was last confined, to Whitehall, where a scaffold had been erected outside the Banqueting House. Charles died bravely, and when his head was severed from his body a great groan went up from the assembled crowd, many of whom pressed forward to dip their handkerchiefs in the royal blood. Thus began the cult of the 'Martyr King', which still has its following today.

The king's body was taken to Windsor for burial in St George's Chapel on 7 February 1649. Charles was one of England's most artistically cultured kings, delighting in collecting works of art and patronising artists. He amassed a collection of some 1,400 paintings and 400 sculptures, many still in the Royal Collection. His portraits by Van Dyck have made his face almost as familiar as that of Henry VIII.

Queen Henrietta Maria had, for safety's sake, left the king at Oxford and made her way to Exeter, where she gave birth to her ninth and youngest child, Henrietta, on 16 June 1644. Soon afterwards she escaped to France, leaving the baby behind in safekeeping, and was well received at the French court. Gradually most of her surviving children were able to join her and she was able to care for them. On the Restoration in 1660 she returned to England as Queen Mother. Pepys, who saw her in November, described her as a 'very little plain old woman'. She was only 51 but her troubles had aged her. Finding English life uncongenial and the climate damaging to her health, she returned to France for good in June 1665. She died at Colombes, near Paris, on 31 August 1669, probably from a massive overdose of opium taken to relieve the pain of cancer. She was buried in the royal basilica of St Denis, where her tomb was despoiled during the French Revolution.

CHARLES II
(1649) 1660–85

Charles, the second son of Charles I and Henrietta Maria, was born at St James's Palace on 29 May 1630. His parents' first child, also named Charles, had been born prematurely at Greenwich in the preceding May after the queen had been frightened by a mastiff jumping at her. The baby had died almost at once, so there was great rejoicing when a strong, healthy heir was born.

Charles was declared Prince of Wales in 1638 but was never formally created so by patent. His education was confided to the Earl (later Duke) of Newcastle and Dr Brian Duppa, Bishop of Chichester, later replaced by Dr John Earle. They did not cram his head full of learning, as had been the fashion in Tudor times, but gave him a good grounding of general knowledge and plenty of sensible advice on everyday life. He was also tutored in mathematics by Thomas Hobbes.

70. *Charles II in Garter robes, a portrait probably from the studio of John Michael Wright, c. 1660–65.*

71. Catherine of Braganza, Charles II's queen, here portrayed in Portuguese court dress, which seemed very strange to English eyes, in a painting by or after Dirk Stoop, c.1660–61.

72. Eleanor (Nell) Gwyn (1650–87) by Simon Verelst, c.1670. Charles II's popular English mistress, Nell Gwyn is said to have been instrumental in persuading the king to found the Royal Hospital in Chelsea for army pensioners.

*73. Charles II's French mistress,
Louise de Kéroualle, whom he created Duchess of
Portsmouth, by Pierre Mignard, 1682. She acted as a spy
for Louis XIV and was most unpopular in England.*

Charles was only 12 years old when he and his younger brother James accompanied their father at the battle of Edgehill, where they narrowly escaped capture. He remained at his father's side throughout most of the Civil War and towards the end of it managed to escape to France, later moving to Holland, where his sister Mary was married to the Prince of Orange. His father's execution in 1649 made him de jure King Charles II and in 1650 he landed in Scotland, raised an army of 10,000 men and after being crowned king of Scots at Scone on 1 January 1651, marched into England, only to suffer an overwhelming defeat by Cromwell at the battle of Worcester. A price of £1,000 was put on his head and he became a fugitive for six weeks (the romantic story of his hiding in an oak tree at Boscobel House belongs to this period), eventually making his escape to France.

The next eight years were passed in exile in France, Germany and Holland, engaged in plotting and planning and attempting to raise money for a future expedition. Meanwhile, Cromwell ruled in England as Lord Protector until his death on 3 September 1658, when he was succeeded in that office by his son Richard. The younger Cromwell had no stomach for government and in May 1659 was compelled to resign by the army, leaving the way open to negotiate Charles's restoration. The prime mover in the matter was General Monck (later Duke of Albemarle) and the outcome was the triumphant return of Charles, who entered London on his 30th birthday, 29 May 1660. He was crowned at Westminster Abbey on 23 April 1661 by William Juxon, Archbishop of Canterbury, who (as Bishop of London) had attended his father on the scaffold. The regalia had been broken up and melted down under the Commonwealth so a new set had to be made for the occasion.

Charles proved himself an astute and pragmatic ruler; the Earl of Rochester's often quoted lampoon that 'he never said a foolish thing, nor ever did a wise one' is largely untrue. His foreign policy, however, left something to be desired as he became very much the tool of France, concluding the Secret Treaty of Dover with Louis XIV in 1670. Shortage of money was a crucial problem as always, and Dunkirk was sold to France for £400,000. In 1672 a Dutch fleet sailed up the Medway and fired British warships at Chatham, greatly damaging the country's prestige abroad, but peace was concluded in 1674.

Charles was married at Portsmouth on 21 May 1662 to the Portuguese Infanta, Catherine of Braganza, daughter of John IV, King of Portugal. She was born at Vila Viçosa, near Lisbon on 25 November 1638 and brought with her as dowry £300,000 and the naval bases of Tangier and Bombay. Sadly, however, she proved barren and was unable to carry a child to full term, miscarrying during the early stages of pregnancy on more than one occasion.

Although having no issue by his queen, Charles, a man as fascinating to the ladies as they were to him, fathered a large progeny – eight sons and five daughters – by his many mistresses, who included Lucy Walter, Barbara Villiers, Duchess of Cleveland, Louise de Kéroualle, Duchess of Portsmouth, and the actress Nell Gwyn. Most of his illegitimate offspring were recognised and ennobled by their father and the present Dukes of Buccleuch, Grafton, Richmond and St Albans are descended from sons of Charles. One woman who resisted his advances was Frances Stewart, Duchess of Richmond, who is said to have modelled the figure of Britannia, which appeared on the reverse side of the coinage for the first time in Charles's reign.

Two domestic events overshadowed Charles's reign: the Great Plague of London in 1665 and the Great Fire in the following year, in which Charles himself helped to fight the flames and displayed great personal bravery. The fire was a blessing in disguise, for it served to clear many of the insanitary and rat-infested areas of the City which had bred the plague and gave scope for the rebuilding of St Paul's Cathedral and many city churches by the brilliant and innovative architect Sir Christopher Wren. Charles was in fact a great patron of the arts and sciences and the founder of the Royal Society. He also founded the Royal Hospital in Chelsea as a home for army pensioners.

The Habeas Corpus Act was passed in Charles's reign and parliamentary government began to develop the party system, Whigs and Tories emerging for the first time.

On 2 February 1685 Charles, who was 54, suffered an apparent stroke at Whitehall. He rallied and lingered until 6 February, when he died after apologising for having been 'an unconscionable time dying'. The real cause of his death appears to have been uraemia. He was received into the Roman Catholic Church on his deathbed, but was buried in Westminster Abbey with Anglican rites. He was, as the diarist John Evelyn summed up, 'A Prince of many Virtues, and many great Imperfections'.

Queen Catherine remained in England until the reign of William and Mary, when, finding she did not get on well with them, she decided to return to Portugal. She made a leisurely journey through France and Spain, arriving in Lisbon in January 1693. In the last year of her life, she acted as Regent of Portugal for her brother King Pedro II, who had grown weary of reigning. She died of a sudden attack of 'colic' at the Palace of Bemposta in Lisbon on 31 December 1705 and was buried in the monastery of Belém.

JAMES II
1685–88

The third, but second surviving son of Charles I and Henrietta Maria was born at St James's Palace on 14 October 1633 and was designated Duke of York from his birth, although not formally so created until 1643.

With his brother Charles he accompanied their father in the campaigns of the Civil War and was handed over to Parliament on the surrender of Oxford in 1646. Two years later he managed to escape to Holland and after Charles II's defeat at Worcester, volunteered to serve in the French army and later in the Spanish. He was a brave soldier and a good commander and gave loyal service to those for whom he fought.

James shared his elder brother's strong sexuality, but his penchant was for ugly women and Charles used to say jokingly of some of James's mistresses that they had been given to him as a penance by his confessor. While still in exile he fell madly in love with the very plain Anne Hyde, a maid of honour to his sister the Princess of Orange and the daughter of Edward Hyde (later Earl of Clarendon and Lord Chancellor). She was far below James in station but he pledged himself to her in secret at Breda in a ceremony later held to have been a marriage on 24 November 1659. Anne became pregnant in 1660 and when her father discovered this, the story of the 'secret marriage' came out. The king was consulted and insisted on James and Anne being married publicly at Worcester House, London, on 3 September 1660, seven weeks before the birth of their first child, a boy who lived less than a year. Four sons and four daughters were born to the couple altogether, but only two daughters, Mary and Anne, survived infancy. The Duchess of York died at St James's Palace on 31 March 1671.

At the Restoration James was appointed Lord High Admiral of England, Ireland and Wales, and of the towns and marches of Calais, Normandy, Gascony and Aquitaine, as well as Constable of Dover Castle and Lord Warden of the Cinque Ports. He held these honours until the passing of the Test Act in 1673 compelled him to relinquish them as a Roman Catholic, having been received into that faith in 1670. As a naval commander he distinguished himself by winning victories over the Dutch in 1665 and 1672.

James married again, by proxy at Modena on 30 September 1673, Mary Beatrice d'Este, the only daughter of Alfonso IV, Duke of Modena. She was a charming and beautiful girl of 15, less than four years older than her elder stepdaughter, Mary. In the first nine years of her marriage the new Duchess of York gave birth to four children, of whom only one, Isabella, survived more than a few months, and even she died in her fifth year.

74. James II (as Duke of York) with his first wife, Anne Hyde, a portrait by Sir Peter Lely.

In the next few years James was gradually rehabilitated in the offices he had been forced to resign because of his Roman Catholicism, and after serving as Lord High Commissioner to the Parliament of Scotland in 1681, was reappointed Lord High Admiral in 1684.

On the death of Charles II in February 1685, James ascended the throne and, although openly acknowledging his faith, began well by summoning a Parliament and appointing his Protestant brother-in-law Laurence Hyde, Earl of Rochester, as Lord High Treasurer. He also banished Charles II's French mistress, the Duchess of Portsmouth, a known agent of Louis XIV. James and Mary were crowned at Westminster Abbey on 23 April 1685 following the Anglican rite (but omitting the communion), having been previously anointed and crowned following the Catholic rite in their chapel at Whitehall on the previous day.

In June, James, Duke of Monmouth, the eldest of Charles II's illegitimate sons, landed at Lyme Regis, claiming the throne as the Protestant champion and alleging that Charles had been secretly married to his mother, Lucy Walter. James's forces were sent against him and he was defeated at Sedgemoor on 5 July. Monmouth was taken prisoner and brought to London, where he begged James for mercy to no avail. He was beheaded in the Tower of London on 17 July. The other rebels were dealt with by the 'Bloody Assizes' of Judge Jeffreys, 230 being executed and several hundred more transported for life, imprisoned, fined or flogged.

James now determined on a course to bring England back to Roman Catholicism and as a first step issued a Declaration of Indulgence removing restrictions imposed on those who did not conform to the established Church of England. Seven bishops (including Archbishop Sancroft of Canterbury, who had crowned the king) protested against this, were imprisoned in the Tower and tried for seditious libel, but all were acquitted on 30 June 1688.

*75. A magnificent terracotta bust of
James II by an unknown artist.*

*76. Mary of Modena, James II's second wife and queen,
a portrait painted by William Wissing at about the
time of their accession to the throne.*

The country might have tolerated James, knowing that his heirs were his daughters, the staunchly Protestant Mary and Anne, but on 10 June 1688 the queen, who had no surviving children, gave birth to a son at St James's Palace. False rumours were at once circulated to the effect that the child was supposititious and had been smuggled into the queen's bed hidden in a warming-pan.

This was widely believed at the time and on 5 November 1688 James's nephew and son-in-law, William, Prince of Orange, landed at Brixham with the avowed intent of safeguarding the Protestant interest and gathered many supporters on his march to London. Deserted on all sides, James panicked. He sent his wife and baby son to France for safety and followed them on 11 December, dropping the great seal of England into the Thames as he was ferried to the boat that was to take him to France. He was apprehended at Sheerness and brought back to Faversham, but a few days later was allowed to make good his escape. Parliament, meeting on 28 January 1689, declared that James had abdicated the throne on the day he first attempted to leave the country.

The exiled king and queen with their baby son settled down at the palace of St Germain-en-Laye near Paris, made over to their use by Louis XIV, and a court in exile was soon set up. James was determined to regain his throne and landed in Ireland with French support in 1689. He held a Parliament in Dublin and remained de facto King of Ireland until defeated by William at the battle of the Boyne on 1 July 1690, when he was forced to withdraw again to France, where he was to spend the rest of his life, planning further invasions and devoting himself to religious observances. A great consolation of his declining years was his daughter Louisa, to whom Queen Mary Beatrice gave birth in 1692.

James died at St Germain from a cerebral haemorrhage on 6 September 1701 and was buried first in the church of the English Benedictines in Paris, but was later removed to the parish church of St Germain, where his tomb was despoiled during the French Revolution.

Queen Mary Beatrice became Queen Regent in exile for her son, the titular 'James III', until he came of age. To her great sorrow, her daughter Louisa died of smallpox in 1712. The queen spent much time at the convent of Chaillot, where the nuns became the recipients of her reminiscences. She died of cancer at St Germain on 7 May 1718, aged 59, and was buried at Chaillot.

WILLIAM III AND MARY II
1689–1702   1689–94

77. *William III in state robes, a portrait attributed to Thomas Murray.*

William Henry, Prince of Orange, was the only child of William II, Prince of Orange, Stadhouder of the United Provinces of the Netherlands, and his wife Mary, Princess Royal (the first to be so entitled), eldest daughter of Charles I. He was born at The Hague on 4 November 1650, eight days after the death of his father.

William was educated at Leyden University and at the age of 17 was admitted to the Council of State of the Dutch Provinces. He paid his first visit to England in 1670, meeting the eight-year-old cousin, Princess Mary, who was later to become his wife. On returning to the Netherlands he was appointed Captain General of the Dutch Forces and later Stadhouder of the United Provinces, an office that had practically become hereditary in his family.

Mary was the eldest daughter and second child of James II and his first wife, Anne Hyde. She was born at St James's Palace on 30 April 1662 and was only 15 years old when she was married in a strictly private ceremony which took place in her bedchamber at St James's Palace at 9 p.m. on 4 November 1677 (William's 27th birthday). Mary was not a happy bride, for apart from the fact that she towered over her short, asthmatic bridegroom, the idea of leaving England appalled her. Nevertheless, the marriage turned out well and Mary adapted to life in Holland, taking an interest in planning gardens and collecting blue and white china. Sadly, Mary miscarried on at least two occasions, and there were to be no children.

On her father's accession to the throne in 1685 Mary became his heiress presumptive and as long as she retained this position James's Catholicism was tolerated by the people. Matters changed in 1688, however, when a son was born to the queen, displacing Mary in the succession. William set out to safeguard the Protestant succession as already related and after James II's flight Mary followed him to London. The throne remained vacant for two months while Parliament pondered the problem. The solution was to offer the throne to William and Mary jointly and they were proclaimed king and queen on 13 February 1689. For their coronation at Westminster Abbey on 11 April several additional pieces of regalia had to be made as well as a duplicate Coronation Chair for Mary. Archbishop Sancroft, who had crowned James II, declined to officiate, so the ceremony was conducted by Henry Compton, Bishop of London.

Mary played little part in public affairs except during William's absences abroad. She was not particularly intelligent and inclined towards Puritanism in religion. Her preferred residences were Hampton Court, which was greatly embellished by Sir Christopher Wren, and Kensington Palace, which was considered good for William's asthma. She was largely responsible for the construction of the Serpentine, the ornamental lake in Kensington Gardens.

78. *Mary II, a portrait by or after William Wissing.*

79.   Queen Anne, as princess, with her son William,
Duke of Gloucester (1689–1700), a portrait from the studio of
Sir Godfrey Kneller, c.1694.

Mary fell ill with smallpox in December 1694. She was dosed with 'Venice treacle', a celebrated panacea of the day containing no fewer than 64 ingredients, but grew progressively worse and died at Kensington Palace on 28 December. Her funeral took place at Westminster Abbey on 5 March 1695 and was attended by members of both Houses of Parliament, a unique occurrence, as hitherto Parliament had always been dissolved on the death of a sovereign. The total cost of the whole ceremony was a staggering £50,000.

After his victory at the battle of the Boyne in 1690 William became a hero to Irish Protestants, who referred to him affectionately as 'King Billy'. The Stuart cause in Scotland was effectively ruined by the death of Dundee, who had won the battle of Killiecrankie for James in 1689, but William's success there was marred by the terrible massacre at Glencoe in 1692. The English naval victory at La Hogue on 19 May 1692 put paid to all chance of direct aid to James from France. On land, however, the French armies were successful and in August 1692 William was defeated at Steinkirk and later at Landen. He retook Namur in 1695, but was unable to win a decisive victory over the French and in 1697 England, France, Holland and Spain agreed the Peace of Ryswick.

William was devastated by Mary's death and continued to reign as sole monarch for the remainder of his life. He was much occupied by the question of the Spanish Succession, although war did not break out until after his death.

After the death of the little Duke of Gloucester, the only surviving child of William's sister-in-law and heiress presumptive, Anne, in July 1700, the Protestant succession was secured by the Act of Settlement, passed in 1701.

William was never popular with his English subjects, who found him too cold and serious. He was opposed by Parliament in his later years and was obliged to cancel grants of land in Ireland made to his Dutch male favourites Keppel and Bentinck. His reign may be said to mark the transition from personal government, as exercised by the early Stuarts, to parliamentary government, which was to come into full flower under the Hanoverians.

In February 1702 William was riding at Hampton Court when his horse stumbled on a mole hill and threw him, breaking his collarbone. After it had been set, he insisted on returning to Kensington Palace by coach. He became feverish a few days later and died of pleuro-pneumonia on 8 March 1702. He was buried in Westminster Abbey. The Jacobites toasted the 'little gentleman in black velvet' (the mole) which had been the cause of William's fatal accident.

ANNE
1702–14

Anne, the second daughter and fourth child of James II and Anne Hyde, was born at St James's Palace on 6 February 1665. She and her elder sister, Mary, were the only two of their parents' eight children to survive infancy and they were brought up together in the Protestant faith of the Church of England, from which neither ever swerved. Anne took after her mother's family, the Hydes, unlike Mary, who was a typical Stuart.

After Mary's marriage to the Prince of Orange, Anne and her stepmother visited the couple in Holland. This visit and one to Brussels two years later were to be Anne's only sorties into continental Europe.

At the age of 17 Anne became the centre of a considerable scandal after John Sheffield, Lord Mulgrave, was suspected of attempting to seduce her. Mulgrave was banished from court and the decision was made to find Anne a husband without delay. In December 1680 the court had been visited by George Louis, Hereditary Prince of Hanover, with a view to a possible union, but the couple formed an antipathy to each other and George returned to Hanover in 1681. No one could have foretold that he would eventually be Anne's successor on the throne.

A more successful suitor was Prince George of Denmark, youngest son of King Frederick III of Denmark, a solid, dull, phlegmatic young man. He and Anne were married in the Chapel Royal at St James's Palace on 28 July 1685. The couple were well matched and their married life a very happy one in spite of Anne's appalling maternity record, 18 pregnancies in 16 years producing only five living children, the longest-lived being William Henry, Duke of Gloucester, who died at the age of 11 in 1700.

Anne and her husband lived at the English court on good terms with her father and stepmother until a son was born to the latter in June 1688. Mary, from Holland, submitted a long questionnaire to Anne seeking the fullest details of the queen's pregnancy and delivery. Most of Anne's answers were evasive and noncommittal and it seems fairly certain that in her own mind she was satisfied that the child was her half-brother.

80. Prince George of Denmark (1653–1708), Queen Anne's dull husband, to whom she was nevertheless devoted, in a portrait after John Riley, c.1687.

After the 'Glorious Revolution' and the accession of William and Mary, Anne became heiress presumptive and on William's death in March 1702 succeeded him as queen. Her health had always been precarious and at her coronation at Westminster Abbey on 23 April she was suffering so badly from gout that she had to be carried in a chair and was unable to stand throughout the ceremony.

Anne was kind and warm-hearted, but like her sister Mary not very intelligent. The people liked her because she had uncultivated tastes and eschewed literature and music, preferring gambling games and stag-hunting in Windsor Forest. Deeply religious, Anne promoted the building of several London churches and established Queen Anne's Bounty, a fund to increase the stipends of the poorer clergy.

Anne had never felt happy about supporting William and Mary against her father, nor about taking the place of her half-brother, and worked hard behind the scenes to try to secure his succession after her. She formed an intense attachment to the masculine-minded Sarah Churchill, Duchess of Marlborough, whose husband's victories abroad were the glory of Anne's reign. Sarah had gained a great ascendancy over Anne before her accession and in letters the two were in the habit of addressing each other as 'Mrs Freeman' (Sarah) and 'Mrs Morley' (Anne) to avoid the otherwise inevitable formality.

On 6 March 1707 the Act of Union between England and Scotland was passed and Great Britain officially came into being. Anne's style was changed from 'Queen of England, Scotland, France and Ireland' to 'Queen of Great Britain, France and Ireland'. In the following year she lost her beloved husband, Prince George, who died at Kensington Palace on 28 October, aged 55.

Anne's health was not helped by her addiction to brandy (her popular nickname was 'Brandy Nan') and it became obvious that her life was not going to be a long one. She fell ill and indolent and her ministers found it hard to obtain her decisions on matters of state. On 30 July 1714 she suffered a stroke at St James's Palace, and a second stroke on 1 August caused her death at the age of 49. She was buried in Westminster Abbey and it was noted that she had become so stout that her massive coffin was almost square.

THE HOUSE OF HANOVER

GEORGE I
1714–27

George Louis, the eldest son of Ernest Augustus, Duke of Brunswick-Luneburg and first Elector of Hanover, and his wife Sophia, fifth and youngest daughter of Frederick V, Elector Palatine of the Rhine and (for one winter) King of Bohemia, and his wife Elizabeth, eldest daughter of James I, was born at the Leineschloss, Hanover, on 28 May (7 June new style) 1660.

George was a strong, sturdy child and his mother took great care over his education and that of his five younger brothers and one sister. He displayed an early bent for a military career and served in the Dutch and Turkish wars. He paid a first visit to England in 1680, but the idea that he might marry his second cousin Anne came to nothing because the young couple developed a strong antipathy towards each other.

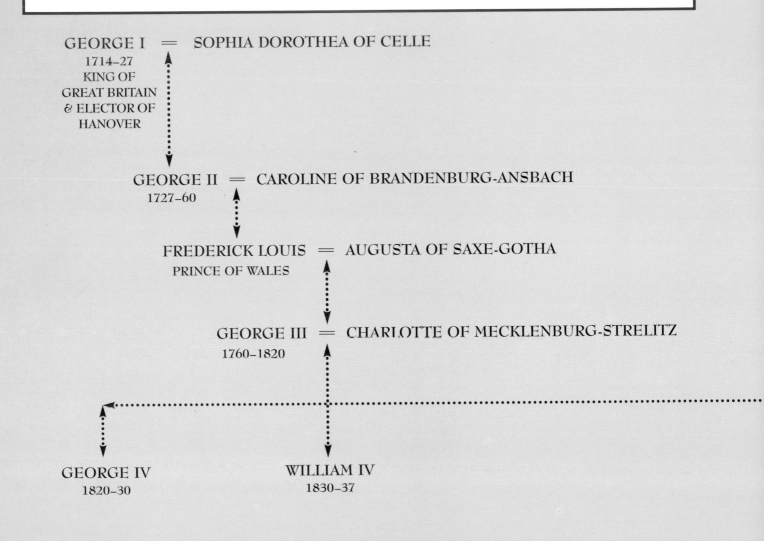

GEORGE I = SOPHIA DOROTHEA OF CELLE
1714–27
KING OF
GREAT BRITAIN
& ELECTOR OF
HANOVER

GEORGE II = CAROLINE OF BRANDENBURG-ANSBACH
1727–60

FREDERICK LOUIS = AUGUSTA OF SAXE-GOTHA
PRINCE OF WALES

GEORGE III = CHARLOTTE OF MECKLENBURG-STRELITZ
1760–1820

GEORGE IV
1820–30

WILLIAM IV
1830–37

81. George I in Garter robes by Sir Godfrey Kneller, 1714.

EDWARD,
DUKE OF KENT & STRATHEARN

VICTORIA = ALBERT OF SAXE-COBURG
1837–1901

EDWARD VII
1901–10

Back in Hanover, George's father arranged for his marriage to his first cousin Sophia Dorothea, only surviving daughter and heiress of George William, Duke of Brunswick-Lüneburg-Celle and his wife Eléonore Desmiers d'Olbreuse, a French Huguenot lady of a rank far inferior to that of her husband. The marriage took place at Celle on 22 November 1682 and was reasonably happy at first, but after the birth of a son and a daughter, the affections of both husband and wife became engaged elsewhere.

George fell in love with one of his mother's ladies-in-waiting, Ehrengard Melusine von der Schulenburg (later to be ennobled in England as Duchess of Kendal), who bore him three daughters (never openly acknowledged as such). Sophia Dorothea, for her part, fell in love with a dashing young officer in the Hanoverian army, Count Philipp Christoph von Königsmarck, who disappeared suddenly in mysterious circumstances in July 1694. His strangled body was reportedly discovered under the floor of the Electoral Princess's dressing-room during alterations to the palace many years later. Incriminating letters from Königsmarck to the princess were found hidden in the lining of some curtains in her apartments. Confronted with this evidence, the fathers of George and Sophia Dorothea agreed that a divorce must be arranged on the grounds of her refusal to continue to cohabit with her husband. A specially convened tribunal of jurists and the Lutheran Church declared the marriage dissolved on 28 December 1694. Sophia Dorothea was removed to the castle of Ahlden in her father's territory and passed the rest of her life there in a not too arduous captivity, receiving visitors and being allowed to drive out in her coach for short distances under escort. She died on 2 November (13 November new style) 1726, aged 60, and was buried with her parents at Celle.

George succeeded his father as Elector of Hanover in January 1698 and three years later his prospects changed dramatically when the Act of Settlement made his mother heiress presumptive to the throne of Great Britain. The Electress Sophia died on 8 June 1714, making George heir presumptive in her place, and on 1 August the death of Queen Anne made him king.

George could speak very little English, although he probably understood more than is generally believed. His preferred language was French and at his coronation at Westminster Abbey on 20 October 1714, the service was largely conducted in Latin to overcome his language difficulties.

82. George II in state robes and exhibiting his well-turned leg, of which he was inordinately proud, in a portrait painted by Thomas Hudson in 1744.

In 1715 the Jacobite rising in Scotland in favour of James II's son 'James III' was soon put down and several of its leaders were executed. George was tolerated rather than popular and the Whigs, with a view to strengthening his support, introduced septennial Parliaments. The king presided over cabinet meetings throughout his reign, the Prince of Wales acting as interpreter where necessary until a rift between father and son developed in 1717.

George was happiest on his frequent visits to his German dominions, and in 1719 these were increased by the cession of the secularised bishoprics of Bremen and Verden. George left for Hanover for the last time in June 1727. On arriving in Holland his coach was waiting for him, and although he had been seasick he set out at once. He spent the following evening at Delden, where he unwisely consumed a large quantity of fruit. The next day a violent attack of diarrhoea forced a halt and when the king returned to his coach it was obvious that he had suffered a stroke. He was bled, but insisted that the journey should continue. The party reached Osnabrück late in the evening and George was carried to his bed, where again he lapsed into unconsciousness. He died at 1.40 a.m. on 22 June 1727, aged 67, and was buried in the Leineschloss Church at Hanover. The church was severely damaged in the Second World War and in 1957 George's sarcophagus and that of his mother were moved to the mausoleum in the grounds of Herrenhausen.

GEORGE II
1727–60

George Augustus, the only son of George I and Sophia Dorothea, was born at Herrenhausen on 30 October 1683. Deprived of their mother's care when he was 11 and his sister Sophia Dorothea (later Queen of Prussia) was seven, the children were brought up with loving kindness by their grandmother, the Electress Sophia. She engaged English tutors for them as soon as she had been declared heiress presumptive in 1701, and George learnt to speak English fluently, although he never lost a strong guttural accent. He was naturalised a British subject in 1705 and created Duke of Cambridge by Queen Anne in the following year, although Anne would never allow him to visit England in her lifetime.

On 22 August (1 September new style) 1705, George was married at Herrenhausen to Caroline, third and youngest daughter of John Frederick, Margrave of Brandenburg-Ansbach, and his second wife, Eleonore Erdmuthe Louise of Saxe-Eisenach. She was seven months older than George, having been born at Ansbach on 11 March 1683. The marriage was very happy, in spite of George's occasional wanderings elsewhere, and produced four sons (of whom only two survived infancy) and five daughters.

83. A charming mezzotint of George II, Queen Caroline, and their seven surviving children. The engraver is unknown.

When George I succeeded Queen Anne in 1714, his son and daughter-in-law accompanied him to London and the younger George was created Prince of Wales and Earl of Chester two days after they had made their state entry. However, a rift between the king and his son occurred in 1717 and in the following year the Prince and Princess of Wales withdrew from court and moved into Leicester House, Leicester Square, which became their principal residence until their succession in 1727.

George and Caroline were crowned at Westminster Abbey on 11 October 1727 and Caroline's dress was so heavily encrusted with jewels that a pulley had to be devised to lift her skirt and enable her to kneel at the appropriate points of the ceremony.

George was a courteous and courtly man, although hasty-tempered, and these qualities were much appreciated by his ministers. Queen Caroline played a greater role in affairs of state than any other queen consort since the Middle Ages. She gave her unqualified support to Sir Robert Walpole, the first prime minister, and relied heavily on her Vice-Chamberlain, Lord Hervey, who sat as Whig MP for Bury St Edmunds for eight years.

The discord that grew between George II and his father was to be repeated to an even greater degree between George and Caroline and their son Frederick Louis, Prince of Wales, whom his mother was to describe as 'the greatest ass, and the greatest liar' that ever lived.

Like his father, George II spent much time in his foreign dominions. He was the last British monarch to lead his men on the field of battle, when the French were defeated at Dettingen in 1743. In 1745 the second Jacobite rising, led by 'Bonnie Prince Charlie', the son and heir of the titular 'James III', was put down with great severity by George's younger son, William, Duke of Cumberland, who earned himself the unenviable nickname of 'Butcher Cumberland'.

Queen Caroline died at St James's Palace on 25 November (1 December new style) 1737, after suffering agonies

84. Caroline of Ansbach, George II's queen, in her coronation robes, which were so heavy that the skirt had to be raised on a pulley. A portrait from the studio of Charles Jervas, c.1727.

from the crude surgery of the day attempting to right an umbilical hernia. On her deathbed she urged the king to marry again. 'Never, never,' he sobbed (in French), 'I shall only have mistresses.'

George's reign was a time of great prosperity at home and abroad. French power in India was destroyed and Canada, Guadeloupe and Senegal were captured. The British Empire was beginning to take shape. The reign also saw the adoption of the Gregorian Calendar in place of the Julian in 1752.

By now the House of Hanover had gained a measure of popularity and support and the earliest version of the national anthem, 'God Save Great George Our King', was first performed when George attended a gala performance at the theatre to celebrate one of Britain's victories. Like his father, George had little interest in the arts, despising all 'boets and bainters', but he had a taste for music and continued the royal patronage of Handel embarked on by his father.

George's elder son, Frederick, Prince of Wales, died suddenly in March 1751, and the heir to the throne for the last nine years of George's reign was Frederick's son George.

On 25 October 1760 the king rose as usual at Kensington Palace and after breakfasting on his customary cup of chocolate entered his water-closet. A few minutes later his valet heard a thud and found the king lying on the floor. He was lifted on to his bed and died within a few minutes, a post-mortem revealing the cause of death as a ruptured aneurysm of the aorta. He was buried beside Caroline in Westminster Abbey and at his direction the sides of their coffins were removed in order that their dust might mingle after death.

GEORGE III
1760–1820

George William Frederick, the eldest son and second child of Frederick Louis, Prince of Wales, and his wife Augusta of Saxe-Gotha, was born at Norfolk House, St James's Square, London, on 4 June 1738. At the time of his birth, George's parents were estranged from his grandfather, George II, and remained so until the Prince of Wales's death in 1751, when the king visited his widowed daughter-in-law and her children to express his condolences and told his grandsons that 'they must be brave boys, obedient to their mother, and deserve the fortune to which they were born'.

A month after his father's death George was created Prince of Wales and Earl of Chester. His education was entrusted to Lord Harcourt and the Bishop of Norwich and his mother played a large part in the formation of his mind and character. When he misbehaved she would admonish him with the words, 'George, be a king!'

85. Augusta, Princess of Wales (1719–72), the mother of George III, here shown as she appeared in her wedding dress in a portrait by Charles Philips, c.1736.

George succeeded his grandfather in October 1760. His mother's great favourite (some said lover) the Earl of Bute was appointed Prime Minister in 1762 and at George's first Opening of Parliament he declared that he 'gloried in the name of Briton', referring to his birth as the first British-born monarch since Anne. In spite of his German antecedents he was the epitome of everything considered British and a living example of the triumph of environment over heredity.

The young king possessed the strong sex drive common to many of his family, but as his equally strong moral principles inhibited him from seeking relief with a mistress he determined to marry as soon as possible. His interest was first aroused by Lady Sarah Lennox, but realising the unsuitability of such a match he set his sights elsewhere and finally chose an obscure German princess, Charlotte of Mecklenburg-Strelitz, youngest daughter of Prince Charles and the niece of the reigning Duke Adolphus Frederick III of Mecklenburg-Strelitz. The 17-year-old Charlotte arrived in England and the marriage took place at St James's Palace on 8 September 1761. Two weeks later, on 22 September, the king and queen were crowned at Westminster Abbey.

Charlotte was no beauty, possessing small simian features, though she was not without a certain charm. She and George, who was tolerably good-looking, settled down to a comfortable and happy married life, producing a large family of 15 handsome children, only two of whom died young. Both king and queen were of very simple habits and tastes and adopted a lifestyle far more akin to that of the rising middle class than to that of the nobility and gentry. Their preferred residences were Kew and Windsor and in 1762 George bought Buckingham House in St James's Park for £21,000. It became known as the Queen's House and only much later, in George IV's time, as Buckingham Palace.

Early in 1764 the king suffered the first attack of an illness now believed to have been the hereditary metabolic disorder porphyria, one of the chief symptoms of which is mental confusion. He recovered quite quickly, but asked Parliament to pass an act enabling him to appoint the queen, or some other member of the royal family, guardian to the heir apparent and regent if the necessity arose. The bill was passed but met with considerable opposition, leading to a change of ministry.

86. Queen Charlotte in coronation robes, a portrait from the studio of Allan Ramsay, 1760s.

George was anxious to break the power of the Whig oligarchy that had ruled the country under the first two Georges and to that end created his own party of 'King's Friends'. Through them he was able to manipulate affairs and effect frequent changes of ministry. He finally appointed his own minister, Lord North, in 1770.

The marriages of two of the king's brothers to ladies he considered entirely unsuitable led to the passing of the Royal Marriages Act in 1772. This provided that no descendants of King George II (with the exception of the descendants of princesses married into foreign families) might contract marriage under the age of 25 without first obtaining the consent of the sovereign in council. Over the age of 25, those wishing to marry without obtaining this consent were obliged to give notice of their intention to do so to the Privy Council and would then be free to marry after a year had elapsed with no objection being raised by either House of Parliament. The Act was to give rise to strange situations affecting some of George's sons and grandsons.

The American War of Independence, resulting in the loss of the American colonies, was a very great blow to the king and in 1788 he suffered his second attack of porphyria. This time it was more serious and he was badly deranged from October to February 1789, when he again made a full recovery.

The events of the French Revolution were a cause of great concern and the last ten years of George's active reign were dominated by the Napoleonic wars in Europe and the threat of invasion. The king entered the 50th year of his reign on 25 October 1809 and a Jubilee was held. His eyesight had been failing since 1805 and the death of his youngest

87. George III in state robes, a portrait from Ramsay's studio, 1760s.

and favourite daughter, Princess Amelia, in 1810 precipitated his last attack of porphyria, from which there was no recovery. The Regency Act was passed and on 11 February 1811 the Prince of Wales was proclaimed Prince Regent of the United Kingdom.

George passed the last years of his life at Windsor Castle, bereft of reason, sight and hearing. He was unaware of the death of Queen Charlotte at Kew Palace on 17 November 1818, and under the care of his second son, the Duke of York, lived on until 29 January 1820, when he died of senile decay at the age of 81, having lived longer than any of his predecessors. He was buried in the new Royal Tomb House, which he himself had commissioned at Windsor.

88. George III in his 80th year, bereft of reason, sight and hearing, a sad portrait of the old king in his martyrdom to porphyria.

GEORGE IV
1820–30

George Augustus Frederick, the eldest son and first child of George III and Queen Charlotte, was born at St James's Palace on 12 August 1762. He was created Prince of Wales and Earl of Chester when he was just five days old.

George was endowed with outstanding good looks, fair hair, blue eyes and a pink and white complexion, although a tendency to corpulence in later life was exacerbated by over-indulgence in food and drink and lack of exercise.

George and his next brother, Frederick, Duke of York, shared an upbringing and education at Kew Palace. George

was an easy learner and acquired a good grounding in literature and science. As he grew up his good looks, high spirits and agreeable manners earned him considerable popularity and made him the darling of the fashionable world, by whom he was nicknamed 'Prinny'. Up to his 18th year the prince met few people apart from his family circle and his tutors, but he then began to associate with the Whig nobility, much to his father's annoyance. He also inherited the strong sex drive of the Hanoverians and a penchant for amply proportioned ladies somewhat older than himself.

On coming of age in 1783 George was given his own establishment at Carlton House, was voted £30,000 by Parliament to pay his debts and received an annual allowance of £50,000 from his father. At about this time he fell in love with a respectable, twice widowed

89. George IV as Prince Regent, a portrait by Sir Thomas Lawrence painted in about 1814.

Roman Catholic lady, Mary Anne (or Maria) Fitzherbert. The only way he could get her was by marriage and on 21 December 1785, having impressed the lady by stabbing (or pretending to stab) himself to show the extent of his passion for her, he persuaded her to take part in a marriage ceremony with him at her house in London. As it contravened the terms of the Royal Marriages Act, it was null and void in law. Had it not been illegal, George, through marriage to a Roman Catholic, would have forfeited his position as heir to the throne under the terms of the Act of Settlement. Rumours of the marriage were soon all over London and the prince took the step of getting his friend Charles James Fox to deny it in the House of Commons.

90. Caroline of Brunswick, a portrait by James Lonsdale showing her at about the time of her husband's accession.

Lavish expenditure on Carlton House involved George in debts amounting to more than £250,000 and he applied to his father, who refused to help him. He accordingly sold off his racehorses, cut down the number of his servants and announced his intention of living in retirement until he had liquidated his debt. The good impression this created paid off. The king agreed to add £10,000 per annum to George's income out of the civil list and Parliament voted a further £161,000 to satisfy creditors and £20,000 for the completion of Carlton House. George at once plunged into a new round of extravagance, including the construction of Brighton Pavilion, his princely pleasure dome in Sussex.

George III's first prolonged attack of madness in 1788 brought the question of the Prince of Wales's possible regency to the fore, and pressures were put on him to marry. By 1794 George's creditors were pressing him again and the promise of a settlement and an increase of income led him to agree to a marriage with his first cousin Princess Caroline of Brunswick, daughter of Charles, Duke of Brunswick, and his wife, Augusta, the eldest sister of George III. The couple took an instant dislike to each other at their first meeting, but the marriage went ahead as arranged and was solemnised in the Chapel Royal, St James's Palace, on 8 April 1795. George only got through the ceremony by being drunk and, as Caroline was later to report, spent his wedding night lying insensible in the grate. The marriage was consummated, however, and on 7 January 1796 Caroline gave birth at Carlton House to a daughter, Princess Charlotte Augusta.

After the baby's birth George sent Caroline proposals for a separation, to which she readily agreed. A dispute over the custody of their child in 1804 was settled by the king undertaking her guardianship. George returned to Mrs Fitzherbert, but was distracted by other mature ladies from time to time.

George III's final descent into madness led to the Prince of Wales being proclaimed Prince Regent on 5 February 1811. The Regency was a brilliant period in British history. It saw the final defeat of Napoleon at Waterloo in 1815 and gave the Regent a chance to indulge his love of splendour by the lavish entertainment extended to the Emperor of Russia, the King of Prussia and other allied sovereigns when they visited England in the course of their triumphant victory progress.

A great blow fell on 6 November 1817, when George's daughter Charlotte, who had been happily married for a year and a half to Prince Leopold of Saxe-Coburg-Saalfeld, died in childbirth after being delivered of a stillborn son. The sad event led to a hasty scramble for marriage among George's younger unmarried brothers, as there was no heir to the throne in the next generation.

The death of George III brought the Regent to the throne as King George IV on 29 January 1820. His first concern was to find a way to prevent his estranged wife, Caroline, who had been travelling abroad for some years, from returning to England to take up her position as queen. All attempts to persuade her to do so having failed, George forced his ministers to bring in a Bill of Pains and Penalties to deprive her of the title of Queen and effectively to dissolve the marriage. The so-called 'trial of Queen Caroline' followed in the House of Lords and ended with the bill being dropped after its third reading on 10 November 1820.

*91. The so-called 'Trial of Queen Caroline' in the House of Lords, by Sir George Hayter, 1820–23.
The queen can be seen seated in the centre.*

*92. A scurrilous caricature by Cruikshank of Queen Caroline
on the arm of her alleged lover Bartolomeo Pergami.*

George planned his coronation at Westminster Abbey on 19 July 1821 to be the most magnificent ever staged. No provision was made for the coronation of Caroline, however, and her pathetic attempts to gain admission to the abbey ended in failure. This final humiliation exacerbated the chronic bowel trouble from which she had suffered for some years and she died at Hammersmith on 7 August 1821. Her body was taken to Brunswick for burial.

George visited Ireland, Hanover and Scotland in the early years of his reign, and was the first monarch since the Stuarts to visit Scotland. His reign saw many changes of ministry and the most important event towards its end was the Catholic Emancipation Act, passed in 1829, despite the king doing his best to block it.

George divided his time between Brighton and Windsor, living very quietly with his last mistress, Lady Conyngham. A serious decline in his heath began in January 1830 and he died on 26 June. He was buried in the Royal Tomb House. His unofficial widow, Mrs Fitzherbert, was treated with great kindness by William IV, who offered to create her a duchess; this she refused, although she accepted the privilege of dressing her servants in the royal livery colours of red and gold. She died in her house at Brighton on 27 March 1837 and was buried in the Roman Catholic Church of St John the Baptist in Brighton.

WILLIAM IV
1830–7

William Henry, the third son of George III and Queen Charlotte, was born at Buckingham House, St James's Park, on 21 August 1765. He was destined for a naval career and went to sea at the age of 14 as an ordinary able seaman, serving at the relief of Gibraltar in 1779. A year later he was promoted midshipman, but on his father's orders received no special privileges. He was present at Cape St Vincent and was stationed in the West Indies and off Nova Scotia. After seeing action off the Delaware in 1782, he joined Lord Hood in quest of the French fleet and formed a friendship with Nelson, under whom he later served in the Leeward Islands as captain of the Pegasus. On 22 March 1787 Prince William undertook the pleasant duty of giving away the bride when Nelson married Mrs Frances Nisbet, a doctor's widow. The following winter the prince returned to England and was appointed to command the frigate Andromeda, returning for a short time to the West Indies.

On 20 May 1784 William was created Duke of Clarence and St Andrews and Earl of Munster by his father and subsequently took his seat in the House of Lords. The following year saw his appointment as Rear Admiral of the Blue and the end of his active service afloat.

At about this time William formed a deep attachment to the actress Dorothea Bland, known professionally as 'Mrs Jordan', and they settled down to a life of domestic bliss that was to endure for 20 years and produce ten children, whom he acknowledged and later, after his accession to the throne, ennobled. They bore the surname of FitzClarence and the eldest son was created Earl of Munster, one of his father's titles before his accession.

In 1811 William was appointed Admiral of the Fleet and in 1814 escorted Louis XVIII back to France, but his happy life with Mrs Jordan ended abruptly in the same year for reasons that have never been clear. She was generously provided for, but the separation was a great blow to her and she suffered a complete physical and mental breakdown, eventually dying in distress at St Cloud in France in July 1816. William's conduct in the matter seems to have been out of keeping with his kindly and generous nature, although it might have been expected from almost any of his brothers.

93. Maria Fitzherbert (1756–1837),
the unacknowledged wife of George IV.

94. Princess Charlotte (1796–1817) and her husband,
Prince Leopold of Saxe-Coburg (later first King of the
Belgians, 1790–1865), depicted in a theatre box
during their idyllic but short-lived marriage.

95. William IV in naval uniform, by Sir Martin Archer Shee, c.1800.

96. Queen Adelaide, by Sir William Beechey, c.1831.

The death of Princess Charlotte in 1817 prompted the unmarried sons of George III to find brides and beget heirs to the throne. William's eventual choice was Princess Adelaide of Saxe-Meiningen, elder daughter of George I, reigning Duke of Saxe-Meiningen, and his wife, Princess Louise Eleonore of Hohenlohe-Langenburg. Although she was William's junior by 27 years, having been born on 13 August 1792, she proved an excellent choice. She travelled to England with her mother and the wedding took place at Kew Palace in the presence of the ailing Queen Charlotte on 13 July 1818. Unfortunately, the desired outcome of the marriage was not achieved, as Adelaide's two daughters both died in infancy and two other pregnancies terminated in miscarriages (one of male twins). Adelaide found solace in mothering William's children and grandchildren by Mrs Jordan, as well as their joint nephews and nieces. She was an admirable woman and she and William became deeply attached to each other.

The death of George III in 1820 placed William second in line to the throne and the death of his elder brother, Frederick, Duke of York, in 1827 made him heir presumptive and gave him an increase in income of £40,000 per annum. He was also appointed Lord High Admiral of England, a post specially revived for him, but resigned the office after the Duke of Wellington raised objections to the expense of his progresses.

William became King William IV on the death of George IV in June 1830. He and Adelaide were crowned at

97. Queen Victoria and Prince Albert with their five elder children,
a charming composition by Franz Xaver Winterhalter painted in 1846.

Westminster Abbey on 8 September 1831 in a ceremony shorn of much of its traditional splendour (including the banquet in Westminster Hall) for the sake of economy.

William had become a garrulous and eccentric old man, given to impetuous outbursts which Queen Adelaide did her best to curb. He could, however, be shrewd and statesmanlike on occasion. His reign was fraught with difficulties. Wellington's administration was followed by that of Earl Grey, who brought in the Reform Bill. After its first rejection by the House of Lords, the king resolutely refused to create new peers to form a Whig majority but sent round a circular letter to the Tory peers, as a result of which 100 of them abstained from voting so that the bill became law.

The personal tastes of the king and queen, like those of his parents, were extremely simple. Unlike his brother and predecessor, William had no interest in the arts and it was said of him that 'he would not know a picture from a window-shutter'. However, he did found the Royal Library at Windsor, not because he was a bibliophile, but because he felt the castle should have one, most of George III's books having gone to form the nucleus of what is now the British Library.

William was fond of his niece and heiress presumptive Princess Victoria, but loathed her mother, the Duchess of Kent, openly expressing his wish that he might live long enough to see Victoria come of age and thus avoid the possibility of the duchess becoming regent. His wish was granted. He died very peacefully at Windsor Castle from pneumonia on 20 June 1837 with his head resting on Queen Adelaide's shoulder, and was buried in the Royal Tomb House.

Queen Adelaide came to enjoy great popularity in the days of her widowhood. She devoted herself to many charitable works and founded and endowed the Anglican Cathedral of St Paul at Valletta, Malta, in 1839. Her health, however, was precarious and she lost the use of one lung. In 1848 she took a lease on Bentley Priory, near Stanmore, Middlesex, from the Marquess of Abercorn and died there on 2 December 1849. She was buried with William in the Royal Tomb House.

VICTORIA
1837–1901

Alexandrina Victoria was the only child of Prince Edward, Duke of Kent (himself the fourth son of George III), and his wife Princess Victoria of Saxe-Coburg-Saalfeld, whose brother Leopold had been the husband of Princess Charlotte of Wales. She was born at Kensington Palace on 24 May 1819 and received her first name in honour of her godfather, Emperor Alexander I of Russia.

Victoria was eight months old when her father died at Sidmouth, Devon, on 23 January 1820, only six days before his father, George III. His widow and daughter were brought back to Kensington Palace by Prince Leopold, who became a father figure to the princess as well as providing financial help to his almost destitute sister. Victoria had no young companions as her half-brother and half-sister, Prince Charles and Princess Feodora of Leiningen, children of her mother's first marriage, were considerably older. Her governess from babyhood onwards was Louise Lehzen, later created a Hanoverian baroness, who was to remain with her until after the queen's marriage, when her jealousy and capacity for mischief-making made her fall foul of Prince Albert and brought about her dismissal.

At the age of eight Victoria was given a tutor, the Rev George Davys (later Bishop of Peterborough), with whom she had daily lessons. She also had French and German tutors, a writing and mathematics master, and a drawing master, Richard Westall, RA, who found her greatly talented. She also enjoyed lessons in dancing, music and singing.

On the accession of William IV in 1830 Victoria became heiress presumptive and her mother took her on a series of 'royal progresses' throughout the country, but incurred the king's displeasure by not allowing her to appear at court as often as he wished. Victoria came of age on her 18th birthday and one month later the death of William IV brought her to the throne. She was crowned at Westminster Abbey on 28 June 1838 and recorded her own impression of the ceremony in her diary.

Prince Leopold had been elected King of the Belgians in 1831, but Victoria was to find another father-figure in her first prime minister, Lord Melbourne, upon whom she came to rely heavily. The greatest male influence in her life, however, was to be her husband and first cousin, Prince Albert of Saxe-Coburg and Gotha, to whom she was married at the Chapel Royal, St James's Palace, on 10 February 1840. The prince was a man of culture and taste, a true polymath, and he moulded and shaped the character of his wife completely. Marriage to Victoria was a full-time occupation, exacting both physically and mentally. When the Prince Consort (as he was created by patent on 26 June 1857) died of typhoid at Windsor Castle on 14 December 1861, aged 42, he had the appearance of a much older man. He left his wife with four sons and five daughters.

Victoria indulged in paroxysms of violent grief after Albert's death. She wore mourning for the rest of her life and refused to undertake any public engagements, earning herself the nickname 'The Widow of Windsor'. Her preferred residences were Osborne House on the Isle of Wight and Balmoral Castle in Scotland, both creations of Prince Albert. In due course she found some comfort in the close relationship she formed with her Highland servant John Brown, a matter of grave concern to her family and household. After Brown's death she formed another close attachment to her Indian secretary, Abdul Karim, known as 'the Munshi', who inspired even more resentment than Brown had done.

In Victoria's reign the British Empire reached the height of its prestige and its apogee was marked by her proclamation as Empress of India at Delhi on 1 January 1877. The new title was a source of great pride and satisfaction to the queen, who felt herself on a par with the Emperors of Russia and Austria and the recently proclaimed German Emperor.

98. A photograph by Mayall of Prince Albert taken on 1 March 1861. Although not yet 42, the cares of office and marriage to Victoria had given the prince the appearance of a much older man.

The queen's relationship with her prime ministers was not always easy. She disliked and distrusted the Liberals and their leader, Gladstone, whom she described as a 'half-mad firebrand'. Lord Palmerston was another prime minister with whom she did not get along. On the other hand, the wily Conservative flatterer Benjamin Disraeli could do no wrong in her eyes.

By the end of her reign Victoria had acquired a popularity greater than that enjoyed by any of her predecessors, and there were great outpourings of affection for her when she celebrated her Golden Jubilee in 1887 and her Diamond Jubilee in 1897.

The queen enjoyed robust health and a hearty appetite throughout her life and only began to fail towards the end of 1900. She spent Christmas at Osborne but continued to sink steadily until she died peacefully, surrounded by her family, on 22 January 1901, after the longest reign in British history. She was buried beside Albert in the Italianate Mausoleum at Frogmore, which she had built to house them both in death.

99. Queen Victoria on her pony with John Brown (1826–83) in attendance, a photograph taken in June 1868 by W. and D. Downey.

100. Victoria, Queen and Empress, a fine photographic study by Bassano, 1887.

THE HOUSE OF
SAXE-COBURG-GOTHA

EDWARD VII ═ ALEXANDRA OF DENMARK
1901–10

⬆
⋮
⬇

GEORGE V
1910–36

EDWARD VII
1901–10

Albert Edward, the eldest son and second child of Victoria and Albert, was born at Buckingham Palace on 9 November 1841. Almost exactly a month later on 8 December he was created Prince of Wales and Earl of Chester and on 17 January 1850 he was further created Earl of Dublin.

Prince Albert devised a careful plan for his son's education, but it soon became evident that he was not a brilliant scholar and lacked diligence. His brothers and sisters were his only companions of his own age and the tutors chosen by his father were for the most part gravely austere and humourless. It was a sad environment for a high-spirited, affectionate boy, but he managed not to be overcome by it and later developed a marked taste for boisterous practical jokes, though it was unwise for his friends to reciprocate.

The prince's parents soon became well aware of the fact that he had inherited the strong sexuality of his Hanoverian great-uncles, as well as that of his paternal grandfather and uncle. Victoria was to attribute the Prince Consort's death in part to a journey he made to Oxford when in a weakened state of health to sort out one of their son's early sexual escapades. This was to be a cause of dissension between mother and son which was never entirely healed and repeated, though to a lesser degree, the relations between the first three Georges and their heirs.

A bride for Bertie, as he was known, was found in the person of Princess Alexandra, eldest daughter of King Christian IX of Denmark and his wife, Princess Louise of Hesse-Cassel, and they were married at St George's Chapel, Windsor, on 10 March 1863. Alexandra, who was born at Copenhagen on 1 December 1844, was extremely beautiful but, as Queen Victoria was to discover, 'sadly deaf'. She was also sexually frigid and after the birth of six children in fairly quick succession, it seems probable that marital relations ceased, although the couple remained on friendly, even deeply affectionate, terms for the rest of their lives together. Alexandra felt no resentment that Bertie found consolation with other ladies, including Lily Langtry, 'Daisy', Countess of Warwick, and the Hon. Mrs George Keppel.

Deprived of any participation in government affairs by his mother, Bertie became a bon viveur in every sense, relishing good food, good wine, good clothes, good cigars and good (sometimes bad) company. He became well known in the fashionable resorts of Europe, Paris, Hamburg, Monte Carlo and Biarritz. He visited Canada and India, where he found kindred spirits in some of the maharajas, who loved to fête him and invite him to shoot tigers from the backs of elephants. Racing and gambling were among his other pleasures.

In 1871 Bertie fell seriously ill with typhoid at Sandringham House, the property in Norfolk which he had bought and rebuilt, and his condition was a cause of grave concern to the queen and the nation. When at length he recovered, the event was celebrated by a thanksgiving service at St Paul's Cathedral.

101. *Edward VII and Alexandra as Prince and Princess of Wales, photographed by Gunn and Stuart of Richmond.*

*102. Lillie Langtry (1852–1929),
the most famous of Edward VII's mistresses,
photographed in 1891.*

*103. Daisy, Countess of Warwick (1861–1938),
another important mistress of Edward VII.*

His mother's death in 1901 brought Bertie to the throne at last, in his 60th year, and he chose to reign as Edward VII. His coronation was arranged to take place on 26 June 1902, but a day or two before the king fell ill with appendicitis and an emergency operation was performed. He made such a rapid recovery, however, that he and Alexandra were crowned at Westminster Abbey with slightly curtailed ceremonial on 9 August.

'King Teddy' enjoyed immense popularity with all classes and his ebullience and bonhomie came as a welcome relief after the drab years of the last half of his mother's reign. He was an able linguist and was well informed on foreign affairs. Enthusiastically pro-French, he supported the gradual rapprochement between France and Britain, culminating in the Entente Cordiale in 1904. This was regarded as largely the result of his efforts, and won him the soubriquet of 'Edward the Peacemaker'.

Long years of self-indulgent good living eventually took their toll on the king and he became a martyr to chronic bronchitis. He died at Buckingham Palace peacefully and fairly suddenly after a short illness on 6 May 1910, and was buried in St George's Chapel, Windsor.

Queen Alexandra was equally popular as Queen Mother and passed her widowhood at Marlborough House and at Sandringham. She died at Sandringham on 20 November 1925, and was buried with Edward; they rest together beneath a tomb bearing their recumbent effigies in medieval style.

104. The Hon. Mrs George Keppel, née Alice Edmonstone (1869–1947),
Edward VII's last and most enduring mistress, was tolerated by Queen Alexandra,
who led her to the king's deathbed to make her farewell.

THE
HOUSE OF WINDSOR

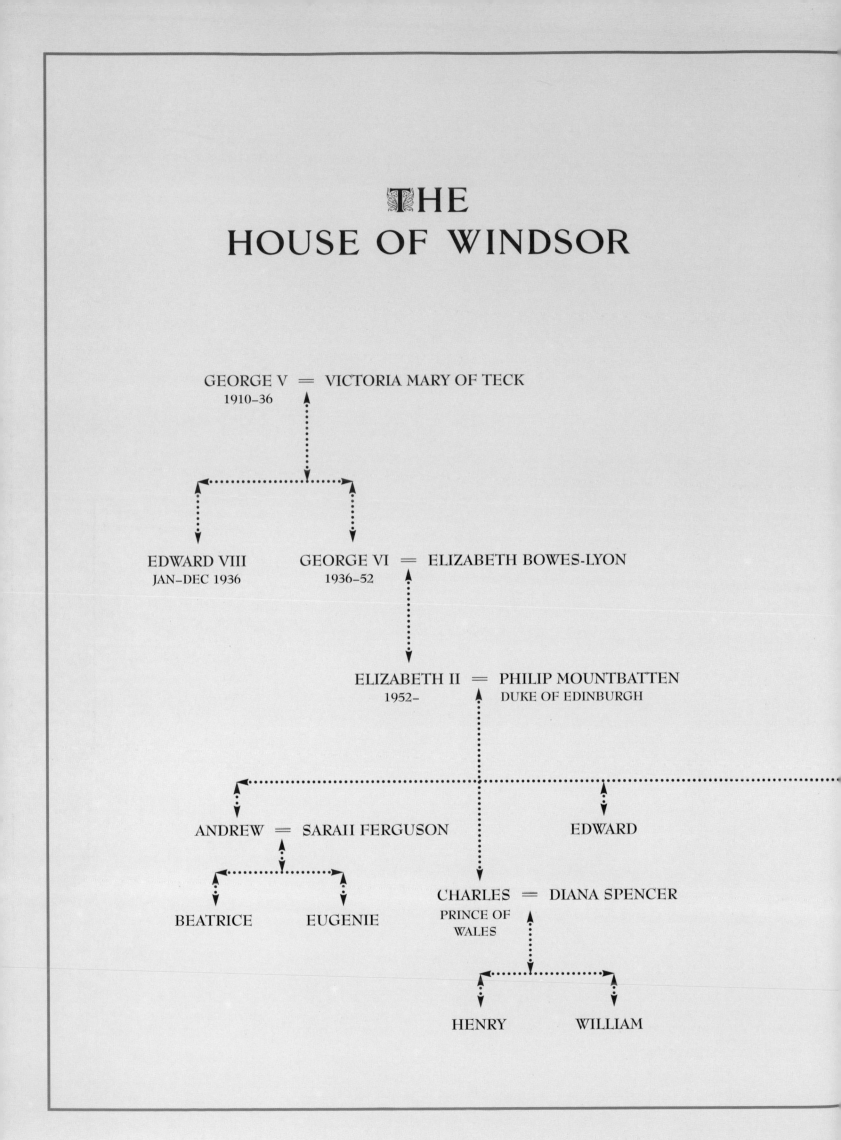

GEORGE V = VICTORIA MARY OF TECK
1910–36

EDWARD VIII   GEORGE VI = ELIZABETH BOWES-LYON
JAN–DEC 1936   1936–52

ELIZABETH II = PHILIP MOUNTBATTEN
1952–   DUKE OF EDINBURGH

ANDREW = SARAH FERGUSON   EDWARD

BEATRICE   EUGENIE   CHARLES = DIANA SPENCER
                               PRINCE OF
                               WALES

HENRY   WILLIAM

105. Queen Elizabeth II by Michael Leonard, 1986.

GEORGE V
1910–36

George Frederick Ernest Albert, the second son of Edward VII and Queen Alexandra, was born at Marlborough House, London, on 3 June 1865.

As the second son of the heir apparent he was able to embark on a naval career, his prospects of succeeding to the throne being remote as he had a healthy elder brother, Albert Victor, who had been born on 8 January 1864. George was therefore able to see more of life at an ordinary level than many princes, and the rough and ready manners of the quarterdeck were to remain with him throughout his life. In this he resembled William IV, although he never aped that king's eccentricities. His brusque heartiness was to endear him to his subjects, so that by the end of his reign he had become one of the best loved and respected of all English monarchs.

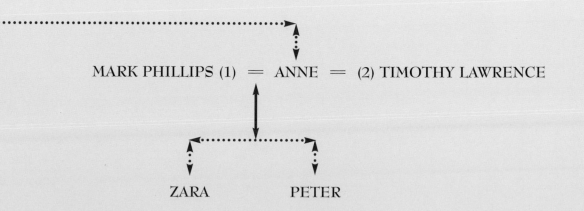

106. A portrait by Sir John Lavery of George V, Queen Mary, the Prince of Wales
and Princess Mary at Buckingham Palace.

George was a devoted son to both his parents and a devoted brother to his siblings. He had a straightforward, uncomplicated mind and was incapable of deviousness in any form. On 14 January 1892 the unexpected death of George's elder brother, Albert Victor, Duke of Clarence, placed him second in line to the throne and his grandmother, Queen Victoria, created him Duke of York. A year later he became engaged to his late brother's fiancée, Princess Victoria Mary of Teck (known in the family as May), the only daughter of Francis, Prince and Duke of Teck, and his wife, Princess Mary Adelaide, daughter of Prince Adolphus, Duke of Cambridge, the seventh son of George III. She was born at Kensington Palace on 26 May 1867, and her marriage to George took place at the Chapel Royal, St James's Palace, on 7 July 1893. The couple were ideally suited and in the course of time became the parents of five sons and one daughter.

The accession of his father in 1901 made George heir apparent and he bore the title of Duke of Cornwall and York until he was created Prince of Wales and Earl of Chester on 9 November 1901. He succeeded to the throne as King George V on his father's death in 1910 and he and Queen Mary (as May decided to be styled) were crowned at Westminster Abbey on 22 June 1911. Later in the year they travelled to India to hold the great Delhi Durbar and receive the homage of the Indian princes. It was a unique occasion, never to be repeated.

In 1914 the world was plunged into the Great War, which was to bring about the biggest change in the old order of things since the Napoleonic wars a century earlier. Britain weathered the storm and the Empire survived, although it was clear that the days of colonialism were numbered. It is doubtful, however, if George V ever realised this. One result of the war was the change of the royal family surname from Saxe-Coburg (or Wettin) to Windsor in 1917 in response to anti-German feeling.

In the years succeeding the war the king continued to impress his people with his sense of duty towards Parliament and the country, accepting the first Labour government with good grace, whatever misgivings he might have felt.

In 1935 King George celebrated the Silver Jubilee of his reign and was greatly moved by the spontaneous demonstrations of love and respect with which he and Queen Mary were met on all sides. It marked a fitting end to his reign. For several years he had battled with respiratory troubles and after spending Christmas at Sandringham he developed a severe bronchial infection and died peacefully on 20 January 1936. He was buried in St George's Chapel, Windsor.

Queen Mary, both as Queen and Queen Mother, was immensely respected for her regal bearing and fortitude. She was destined to live through the reigns of her two eldest sons, Edward VIII and George VI, the abdication of the former, the Second World War in the reign of the latter, and to die at Marlborough House early in the reign of her granddaughter Elizabeth II on 24 March 1953. She was buried beside George and their tomb at the west end of the nave of St George's Chapel is the last to bear recumbent royal effigies in medieval style.

EDWARD VIII

January–December 1936

Edward Albert Christian George Andrew Patrick David, the eldest son of George V and Queen Mary, was born at White Lodge, Richmond Park, Surrey, on 23 June 1894. At his birth he occupied the unique position of being the third male heir in direct line to the throne.

On his father's accession in 1910 he became heir-apparent and was created Prince of Wales and Earl of Chester on 2 June 1910. He was formally invested as such at Caernarvon Castle on 13 July 1911 in a ceremony largely devised by Lloyd George, for which he was required to wear what he considered to be a ridiculous fancy dress, which caused him to chafe at all royal ceremonial and protocol thereafter.

107. *A photograph by Dorothy Wilding of the Duke and Duchess of Windsor, taken in 1955.*

108. Conversation Piece at the Royal Lodge, Windsor.
George VI, Queen Elizabeth and their daughters, Princesses Elizabeth and Margaret,
by Sir James Gunn, 1950.

David (as the Prince of Wales was known in the family) was educated at the Royal Naval College and at Magdalen College, Oxford, and on the outbreak of the First World War was anxious to see active service on the front line, but was forbidden to do so by his father, in spite of the prince pointing out that as he had four younger brothers his life could be put at risk.

In the 1920s and 1930s David made several overseas tours, where his good looks, ready charm and general affability made a great impression. He gained a great following at home and aboard and was considered an arbiter of fashion and a trend-setter, much to the disgust of his father, who set no store by such things. He showed no sign of wanting to marry and settle down and it soon became obvious to his intimates that his taste, like that of an earlier Prince of Wales (George IV), was for mature married ladies, although David preferred them to have thin, boyish figures in the prevailing fashion. A succession of ladies occupied his attention, but by the mid-1930s it became evident in court circles that his affections had been permanently engaged by the American Mrs Wallis Simpson, who lived in London with her businessman second husband Ernest Simpson. David and Wallis first met at a house party at Melton Mowbray in January 1931, and thereafter the Simpsons became frequent guests at Fort Belvedere, the house near Windsor which David had persuaded his father to give him, and Wallis often acted as the prince's hostess in spite of the complacent presence of her husband.

By the time David succeeded his father as King Edward VIII in January 1936, he was completely besotted with Wallis and with almost incredible naïvety was convinced that once she was freed of her marriage he would be able to marry her and make her queen.

For the sovereign head of the Church of England to marry a twice-divorced woman was unthinkable to the Establishment and the king's insistence on going ahead with his plans in spite of all advice provoked a government crisis. Finding that a compromise was impossible, the king abdicated in favour of his brother the Duke of York after a reign of nearly 11 months on 10 December 1936. The following day he made a farewell broadcast to the nation and left the country.

Wallis's divorce from Ernest Simpson was concluded, and on 3 June 1937 she and David were married in France. On 8 March he had been created Duke of Windsor by his brother and successor George VI and on 27 May had received 'reconferment' of the style of Royal Highness by Letters Patent, expressly stating that this was for himself personally and could not be extended to his wife or any children. The legality of this was extremely doubtful. As the son of a sovereign, David was entitled to the style, which should have reverted to him automatically on his renunciation of the throne, while the limitation now imposed was completely unconstitutional. David was to chafe under this injustice for the rest of his life, but out of deference to his brother never made an open issue of it, although within his own household the Duchess of Windsor was always addressed as 'Royal Highness'.

The Duke was still anxious to serve his country in any capacity he might be called upon to fill, but apart from a short wartime tour of duty as Governor and Commander-in-Chief of the Bahamas from 1940 to 1945, the rest of his life was lived out in the obscurity of a self-imposed exile in France, participating with his wife in an endless social round. He wrote a volume of memoirs, *A King's Story*, and two other books of royal reminiscences, and his wife produced her version of events under the title *The Heart Has its Reasons*.

The former king died of cancer at his residence in the Bois de Boulogne on 28 May 1972. His body was brought back to England for a lying-in-state and funeral at St George's Chapel, Windsor, followed by interment in the royal burial ground at Frogmore. His widow lived on for nearly 14 years in an increasing state of senile dementia until she died in Paris on 24 April 1986. Her body, too, was brought back to England and buried beside his.

GEORGE VI
1936–52

Albert Frederick Arthur George, the second son of George V and Queen Mary, was born at York Cottage, Sandringham, on 14 December 1895, his birth on the anniversary of the death of the Prince Consort causing some distress to his great-grandmother, Queen Victoria. In the family the new prince was always known as Bertie.

As a second son with little prospect of succeeding to the throne, Bertie entered the Royal Navy as a midshipman in 1913 and, unlike his elder brother, was allowed to see active service during the First World War with the Grand Fleet. He distinguished himself at the battle of Jutland in 1916 and was mentioned in despatches. He ended the war with the Royal Naval Air Service.

The prince was never robust and in addition to a speech impediment, which he strove hard to overcome, he suffered gastric complaints which necessitated operations for appendicitis and a duodenal ulcer.

On 3 June 1920, Bertie was created Duke of York, and soon after he started the Duke of York's Camps, a scheme for bringing together public schoolboys and working-class boys in seaside holiday camps. These were a great success and were held annually until 1939.

The duke developed a close friendship with Lady Elizabeth Bowes-Lyon, born on 4 August 1900, the youngest daughter of the 14th Earl of Strath-more and Kinghorne and his wife, Nina Cecilia Cavendish-Bentinck. She was a bridesmaid to his sister Princess Mary in 1922 and in January 1923 she and Bertie announced their engagement. They were married at Westminster Abbey on 26 April 1923. In the course of the next seven years two daughters were born and the Duke and Duchess of York settled down to a happy family life, as well as serving the country by carrying out official duties and making Commonwealth tours.

When the abdication of Edward VIII made Bertie king in December 1936, he felt himself to be entirely unfitted for the role. He assumed the style of George VI and with the support of his wife and family manfully assumed his new duties. George VI and Queen Elizabeth were crowned at Westminster Abbey on 12 May 1937, the day appointed for the coronation of Edward VIII.

Within a few years of George's accession the country was plunged into the Second World War. The example of the king and queen, who refused to leave London throughout the bombing or even send their children to a safe area, did much to boost public morale.

After the war ended in 1945, the king and queen pursued a busy programme, including a strenuous tour of South Africa and patronage of the Festival of Britain in 1951. The king's never very robust health began to cause some concern. In September 1951 part of his left lung was removed and found to be cancerous (although this fact was concealed from him). He made a partial recovery and in January 1952 felt so much better that his daughter Princess Elizabeth was able to set off on a projected world tour without any qualms. On 5 February 1952 the king spent a happy day out shooting at Sandringham, but some time after midnight he died peacefully in his sleep. He was buried at St George's Chapel, Windsor, where a new chantry chapel was constructed for him off the north choir aisle and dedicated in March 1969.

Few monarchs have been as greatly loved as King George VI, a shy, retiring man who never wanted to be king but who shouldered the burdens of sovereignty with courage and dignity.

King George's widow assumed the style of Queen Elizabeth the Queen Mother and has never ceased to command popular admiration and respect. She celebrated her 97th birthday in August 1997 and, incredibly, still carries out a number of public duties which would be exhausting to a much younger person.

ELIZABETH II
1952–

Elizabeth Alexandra Mary, the elder daughter of George VI and Queen Elizabeth, was born at 17 Bruton Street, London W1 (the London residence of her maternal grandparents), on 21 April 1926. She was educated privately and, although intelligent and able, made few pretensions to being an intellectual, preferring such pursuits as riding and amateur drama.

Her father's accession to the throne in December 1936 made Elizabeth heiress presumptive and she and her younger sister, Margaret, attended their parents' coronation the following May.

The greater part of the war years were spent at Windsor Castle. Her father refused her permission to train as a nurse because of her youth, but later she was permitted to join the ATS (Auxiliary Training Service) and learned to drive various kinds of heavy vehicle. After the war the two princesses accompanied their parents on their South

109. Charles, Prince of Wales, by Bryan Organ, 1980.

African tour, in the course of which Princess Elizabeth celebrated her 21st birthday at Cape Town, making a moving broadcast in which she pledged her whole life to the service of the British Commonwealth.

Not long after the royal family's return to England, the princess's engagement to Lieutenant Philip Mountbatten, RN, was announced. He was born at Corfu on 10 June 1921, and like her was a great-great-grandchild of Queen Victoria, being the only son of Prince Andrew of Greece and Denmark and his wife, Princess Alice of Battenberg. Philip had served in the Royal Navy since 1939 and in February 1947 renounced his title of Prince of Greece and Denmark and was naturalised a British subject, taking the surname of Mountbatten, an anglicisation of the German name of his mother's family. The couple were married at Westminster Abbey on 20 November 1947 and on the eve of the wedding Philip was created Duke of Edinburgh and received the style or qualification of Royal Highness, which he had relinquished on his naturalisation. He was not granted the dignity of a prince of the United Kingdom until 1957, however. A son, Prince Charles Philip Arthur George, was born on 14 November 1948, and a daughter, Princess Anne Elizabeth Alice Louise, on 15 August 1950.

In February 1952, while in Kenya, where she was about to start on a world tour, Princess Elizabeth received the news of her father's death. She returned to London as Queen Elizabeth II and was crowned at Westminster Abbey on 2 June 1953.

During the course of her lengthy reign, the queen has set about presenting herself as everything a 20th-century monarch should be, winning praise for her dignified acceptance of her duties and responsibilities and making efforts to communicate with her subjects on a regular basis, while never reducing the mystique of royalty by becoming too familiar. As head of the Commonwealth she has undertaken many strenuous tours all over the world with unflagging enthusiasm.

Two more sons were born to the queen, Prince Andrew Albert Christian Edward on 19 February 1960, and Prince Edward Anthony Richard Louis on 10 March 1964.

An accumulation of problems has grown around the royal family in recent years. Prince Charles, Prince of Wales, was married at St Paul's Cathedral on 29 July 1981 to Lady Diana Spencer, youngest daughter of the 8th Earl Spencer. After the birth of two sons, Prince William Arthur Philip Louis on 21 June 1982 and Prince Henry Charles Albert David on 15 September 1984, the marriage encountered difficulties and the prince and princess separated in 1992. A divorce was finally agreed on and made absolute on 28 August 1996. Diana, Princess of Wales, enjoyed a tremendous popularity, not only for her beauty and vivacity but also for her devotion to many charitable causes and her campaign for the banning of landmines throughout the world. The nation was stunned when she was killed in a motor accident in Paris in the early hours of the morning of 31 August 1997. Her former husband escorted her body back to London and her public funeral at Westminster Abbey was the occasion of an outpouring of public grief and emotion probably greater than anything seen in this country before.

The marriage of the queen's second son, Prince Andrew, Duke of York, also foundered, as did the first marriage of her daughter Anne, Princess Royal, although the latter has remarried.

As these lines are written Queen Elizabeth II is about to celebrate her Golden Wedding and it is to be hoped that there will be happier times ahead.

110. Diana, Princess of Wales (1961–97), by Bryan Organ, 1981.

Allen, D.F. *The Belgic Dynasties of Britain and their Coins* (1944)

Appleby, John T. *The Troubled Reign of King Stephen* (1969)

Ashley, Maurice *James II* (1977)

Barlow, Frank *William I and the Norman Conquest* (1965); *Edward the Confessor* (1970); *William Rufus* (1983)

Battiscombe, Georgina *Queen Alexandra* (1969)

Bede *A History of the English Church and People* (translated by Leo Sherley-Price, revised by R.E.Latham) (1968)

Bingham, Caroline *James I of England* (1982)

Bland, Olivia *The Royal Way of Death* (1986)

Bradford, Sarah King *King George VI* (1989); *Elizabeth – A Biography of her Majesty the Queen* (1996)

Brooke, Christopher *The Saxon and Norman Kings* (1963)

Burke's Guide to the Royal Family (1973)

Chapman, Hester W. *Queen Anne's Son – A Memoir of William Henry, Duke of Gloucester 1689–1700* (1954)

Cheney, C.R. *Handbook of Dates for Students of English History* (1945)

Connell, Neville *Anne* (1937)

Cowles, Virginia *Edward VII and his Circle* (1956)

Davis, R.H.C. *King Stephen* (1967)

Donaldson, Frances *Edward VIII* (1974)

Douglas, David C. *William the Conqueror* (1964)

Ellis, Peter Beresford *Caesar's Invasion of Britain* (1978)

Fraser, Antonia *Mary Queen of Scots* (1969); *King James VI of Scotland, I of England* (1974) *King Charles II* (1979); *The Six Wives of Henry VIII* (1992)

Fraser, Flora *The Unruly Queen – The Life of Queen Caroline* (1996)

Garmonsway, G.N. (translator) *The Anglo Saxon Chronicle* (1953)

Green, David *Queen Anne* (1970)

Greenwood, Alice *Lives of the Hanoverian Queens of England*, 2 vols (1909–11)

Hampden, J. *Crusader King* (1956)

Harvey, John *The Plantagenets* (1948, revised edn 1959)

Hatton, Ragnhild *George I – Elector and King* (1978)

Hedley, Olwen *Queen Charlotte* (1975)

Henderson, P. *Richard Coeur-de-Lion* (1958)

Hibbert, Christopher *Charles I* (1968); *George, Prince of Wales* (1972); *George IV, Regent and King* (1973)

Hobhouse, Hermione *Prince Albert – His Life and Work* (1983)

Holm, Thea *Caroline – A Biography of Caroline of Brunswick* (1979)

Hopkirk, Mary *Queen Adelaide* (1946)

Jones, Michael K. and Underwood, Malcolm G. *The King's Mother – Lady Margaret Beaufort, Countess of Richmond and Derby* (1992)

Kendall, Paul Murray *Richard the Third* (1955)

Keynes, Simon and Lapidge, Michael (translators) *Alfred the Great – Asser's Life of King Alfred and other contemporary sources* (1983)

Lane H.M. *The Royal Daughters of England*, 2 vols (1910)

Leslie, Shane *Mrs Fitzherbert*, 2 vols (1939)

Lofts, Norah *Anne Boleyn* (1979)

Longford, Elizabeth *Victoria R.I* (1964)

Magnus, Phillip *King Edward the Seventh* (1964)

Montague-Smith, Patrick W. *Queen Elizabeth the Queen Mother* (1985)

Morris, John *The Age of Arthur* (1973); *Londinium: London in the Roman Empire* (1982)

Nicolson, Harold *King George V – His Life and Reign* (1952)

Oman, Carola *Mary of Modena* (1962)

Onslow, Earl of *The Empress Maud* (1939)

Panter, Helen *King Edgar* (1971)

Parry, Sir Edward *Queen Caroline* (1970)

Pepys, Samuel *The Diary of Samuel Pepys* (edited by R.C.Latham and W. Mathews) (1972)

Pope-Hennessy, James *Queen Mary* (1959)

Powicke, F.M. *Handbook of British Chronology* (1939)

Quennell, Peter *Caroline of England* (1939)

Rae, James *The Deaths of the Kings of England* (1913)

Rose, Kenneth *King George V* (1983)

The Royal Mausoleum, Frogmore Guide Book (1964)

Salzman, L.F. *Edward I* (1968)

Scarisbrick, J.J. *Henry VIII* (1968)

Smith, L.B. *A Tudor Tragedy – The Life and Times of Catherine Howard* (1961)

Strickland, Agnes *Lives of the Queens of England* (1840–48, revised edition 1869)

Sturdy, David *Alfred the Great* (1995)

Thorpe, Lewis *The Bayeux Tapestry and the Norman Invasion* (1973)

Turner, F.C. *James II* (1948)

Victoria, H.M. Queen *Letters*, edited by A.C. Benson and Viscount Esher (1907)

Warnicke, Retha M. *The Rise and Fall of Anne Boleyn* (1989)

Warren W. L. *King John* (1961)

Wedgwood, C.V. *The Trial of Charles I* (1964)

Weir, Alison *Children of England – The Heirs of King Henry VIII* (1996)

Wheeler-Bennett, J.W. *King George VI* (1958)

Williamson, David *Debrett's Kings and Queens of Britain* (1986); *Debrett's Guide to Heraldry and Regalia* (1992); *Brewer's British Royalty* (1996)

Windsor, H.R.H. The Duke of *A King's Story* (1951)

Woodham-Smith, Cecil *Queen Victoria – Her Life and Times*, Vol 1 1819–1861 (all published) (1972)

Yearsley, Macleod *Le Roy est Mort! An account of the deaths of the rulers of England* (1935)

Ziegler, Philip *William IV* (1971); *King Edward VIII: The Official Biography* (1990)

LIST OF ILLUSTRATIONS

Frontispiece:
Elizabeth II, Prince Philip and their grandchildren
Yousuf Karsh, 1987
Photograph, 97.2 x 73.1cm (38¼ x 28¾")
© Yousuf Karsh, 1987
National Portrait Gallery (P543)

1. Edgar, c.943–75
Stained glass window, All Souls College Chapel, Oxford
Courtesy of the Warden and Fellows of All Souls, Oxford

2. Ethelbert, d.616
Stained glass window, All Souls College Chapel, Oxford
Courtesy of the Warden and Fellows of All Souls, Oxford

3. Oswald, King of Northumbria, c.604–41
Stained glass window, All Souls College Chapel, Oxford
Courtesy of the Warden and Fellows of All Souls, Oxford

4. Eighteenth-century engraving of four early English kings
Portraits and Dresses of the Kings of England
Engraving, 33 x 21.5cm (13 x 8½")
© National Portrait Gallery (ER14678)

5. Athelstan, c.895–939
Stained glass window, All Souls College Chapel, Oxford
Courtesy of the Warden and Fellows of All Souls, Oxford

6. Alfred the Great, 849–901
Unknown artist, c.887
Silver penny, diameter 1.9cm (¾")
© National Portrait Gallery (NPG 4269)

7. Eighteenth-century engraving of four early English kings
Portraits and Dresses of the Kings of England
Engraving, 33 x 21.5cm (13 x 8½")
© National Portrait Gallery (ER14679)

8. Athelstan, c.895–939
Illuminated manuscript from Bede's *Life of St Cuthbert*, c.930
29.2 x 20cm (11½ x 7⅞")
Courtesy of The Master and Fellows of Corpus Christi College, Cambridge

9. Edred, c.923–55
Unknown engraver after unknown artist
Line engraving, trimmed down
© National Portrait Gallery (RN49477)

10. Edwy, c.941–59
Unknown engraver after unknown artist
Line engraving, trimmed down
© National Portrait Gallery (RN14676)

11. Edgar, c.943/4–75
Illuminated manuscript,
Charter of Edgar to the New Minster, Winchester, 966
MS Cott.Vesp. A.VIII, folio 2, verso
By permission of the British Library

12. Edward 'the Martyr', c.962–79
Unknown engraver, 1776
Line engraving, 24 x 17.5cm (9½ x 6⅞")
© National Portrait Gallery (RN46035)

13. Ethelred 'the Unready', c.968–1016
Illuminated manuscript, *The Chronicle of Abingdon*, c.1220
MS Cott. Claude B.VI folio 87, verso By permission of the British Library

14. Sweyn 'Forkbeard', c.970–1014
Unknown engraver (image taken from a coin)
Etching, 15 x 8.5cm (6 x 3⅜")
© National Portrait Gallery (RN49478)

15. Canute, c.995–1035
Illuminated manuscript, *Liber Vitae*, 1031
Stowe Ms 944, folio 6
By permission of the British Library

16. Edward 'the Confessor', c.1004–66
Cast of wax seal, diameter 7cm (2¾")
By permission of the British Library

17. Harold, c.1022–66
Based on an original by Theodoric, 1066
Silver penny, diameter 1.9cm (¾")
© National Portrait Gallery (NPG 4050)

18. William I, 'the Conqueror', 1027–87
Based on an original by Theodoric, 1068
Silver penny, diameter 1.9cm (¾")
© National Portrait Gallery (NPG 4051)

19. Matilda of Flanders, c.1031–83
Unknown artist
Pen, ink and watercolour, 18 x 13.3cm (7⅛ x 5½")
© National Portrait Gallery (RN49540)

20. William II, 'Rufus', c.1056/60–1100
Rennoldson after Wale (probably Samuel)
Line engraving, 30 x 21cm (11¾ x 8¼")
© National Portrait Gallery (RN49479)

21. Henry I, 1068–1135
Unknown artist, 17th century
Oil on panel, 58.1 x 45.1cm (22⅞ x 17¾")
© National Portrait Gallery (NPG 4980(2))

22. Stephen, c.1096–1154
Unknown artist, 17th century
Oil on panel, 58.1 x 45.1 (22⅞ x 17¾")
© National Portrait Gallery (NPG 4980(3))

INDEX OF KINGS, QUEENS
AND ROYAL FAMILY MEMBERS